The
Philosopher's
Book *of*
Questions
& Answers

Questions to Open Your Mind

✳

Find out how the wise words of
SOCRATES, KIERKEGAARD, DESCARTES, NIETZSCHE,
and more apply to your life

D. E. WITTKOWER, PhD

adamsmedia
Avon, Massachusetts

Published by
Adams Media, a division of F+W Media, Inc.
57 Littlefield Street, Avon, MA 02322. U.S.A.
www.adamsmedia.com

ISBN 10: 1-4405-5886-8
ISBN 13: 978-1-4405-5886-3
eISBN 10: 1-4405-5887-6
eISBN 13: 978-1-4405-5887-0

Printed in the United States of America.

10 9 8 7 6 5 4 3 2 1

*This book is available at quantity discounts for bulk purchases.
For information, please call 1-800-289-0963.*

Contents

INTRODUCTION

Philosophy.

The word itself means "love of wisdom," and this characterizes well what philosophy is and why it is of constant relevance to us. Philosophy doesn't just seek knowledge; it tries to find the meaning and relevance of that knowledge. It seeks not just an understanding of what we are and what the world is, but an understanding of why things are the way they are, what difference it makes, and how we can know what is possible for us to know (and what is not). Philosophy is the mother of all other fields of knowledge—philosophy established the very idea of science, for example, and continues to ask the questions that science cannot answer: how science works, and what its limitations are. The same holds true for psychology, which can tell us a great deal about how the mind works, but stops short of asking what a mind is—here, psychology must return to the most fundamental questions, still within the realm of philosophy. Similarly, political science and economics can tell us many valuable things about the mechanics of governance and the management of social and natural resources, but we have to return to the open and boundless inquiry of philosophy to answer foundational questions about what is just and unjust, and about the moral and human values at stake in our treatment of one another, and of the environment.

Philosophers have played a declining role in our culture during the last century, and philosophers are not known and discussed figures like we have been in centuries past, but philosophical issues have become no less pressing and no less relevant. Too often today we turn to physicists to talk about the nature of reality and to sociologists and politicians to talk about morality—questions that they will gladly admit are not the kinds of things that their tools and techniques are able to answer. Many people, though, still turn to philosophy to answer these philosophical issues, even though philosophers rarely appear on television or in magazines to help work through fundamental concerns of knowledge, morality, and faith.

This book is a contribution to the process of bringing philosophy back into public dialogue and personal exploration. I want to show here how the wisdom of the ancients and the speculation of contemporary philosophers can support your own engagement with the kinds of questions uniquely proper to philosophy: questions for which there are no clear and unambiguous answers, but which are of such great importance that we cannot but attempt to answer them anyhow.

Each entry in the book has two parts: on the first page, a few questions, and on the next, some philosophical discussion of the issues at play in the questions. There are several ways to work through the book. One is to try a daily routine: Sit down with the questions in the morning over coffee, think about them during the day and make time to write about them, and then explore the philosophy in the evening. On the other hand, you may want to sit down to explore an entry at a single sitting, maybe in a coffee shop. (Either way, coffee is obviously recommended.)

Another possibility is a "book club" or "Socrates Café" approach. As indispensable as it is to try to get clarity for yourself in writing, philosophy is best done along with others. Do you have friends whom you like to explore ideas with, or do you enjoy talking through beliefs and perspectives with your partner? Discuss entries together, but be sure to set aside some time for individual writing as well; talking allows you to pass too quickly over complex problems, whereas writing can force you to confront the issues. You could also work through one of the eleven chapters by yourself and then get together with friends, maybe over drinks (besides coffee), to talk about your thoughts and reactions.

The ancient Greeks would get together over wine, present a philosophical issue, and each address it in turn—with some liquid stimulation. The Latin saying is *in vino veritas*—"there is truth in wine"—but I might say more modestly "drink responsibly, but think with abandon."

No matter what approach you take, the book will work best if you go through the entries in order—they build from one to the next to develop different aspects of each topic.

A Note on Content

The topics here are extremely varied but not comprehensive. If you have some background in philosophy, you might notice an emphasis on Continental rather than Analytic or Pragmatic traditions—my own training is very broad, both historically and across these different traditions, but I do favor Continental philosophy and also often found that many exciting ideas in Analytic philosophy were too situated within technical concerns to be able to ask open and easy-to-discuss questions about. You might also notice, among the religious questions, an emphasis on Christianity. This reflects the history of Euro-American philosophy rather than any view of mine or any implied claim about what's important to consider carefully, and I've tried to present things so that these questions are valuable to people of a variety of faiths, or of no faith.

The questions will sometimes be ambiguous. They will sometimes be frustrating, or leading. Some will have easy answers that are hard to explain, whereas some will be difficult to come to grips with. This is on purpose. This isn't a class—there's no right answer that you're supposed to get—and philosophically valuable questions can be valuable precisely because of what you have to go through to get to an answer. In writing these questions, my goal has been to give you a challenge and a direction for thought and discovery. I am not always playing nice, or even playing fair.

The "answers" here are often not answers at all. I think that's appropriate: These issues wouldn't be philosophical issues at all if there were definitive answers. The perspectives I've included were not necessarily chosen because I think they are right, or because I think you'll find them convincing, although that is certainly sometimes the case. They are chosen primarily because they're significant, plausible, and challenging—in short, worth working with and working through.

Enough preliminaries. Have fun.

※

CHAPTER 1

Happiness
and the
Meaning
of Life

The good life was a central concern to the ancient Greeks, and the question of what kind of life was best led them to considerations of virtue, freedom, pleasure, and happiness. In medieval philosophy, these concerns shifted to considerations of sin and salvation. In modern philosophy—and for philosophers the "modern" period starts in the 1600s, with René Descartes often used as a dividing line—the question becomes not "How should one live?" but "How should one act?" and the question of the good life becomes secondary to questions of moral behavior and ethical choices. Still later, especially along with the rise of religious skepticism, agnosticism, and atheism, the question of the meaning of life became pressing.

While that's the shape of the general trend, these questions are obviously connected, and philosophers (and others) have had all of these concerns in all of these different periods. We won't go through them in any historical order. As you'll see, though, once we start pulling on a particular thread, the fabric will bunch up, showing how intertwined these concerns and questions are.

The Epicurean's Wealth

If you had ten times your wealth and ten times your income, what would you do that you can't do now?

_____

_____

_____

_____

What's a version of that activity that you could do right now?

_____

_____

_____

Is it ten times less meaningful, important, or enjoyable than the activity you would do with more money? Why or why not?

_____

_____

_____

_____

The Philosophy

What do we want money for? Maybe you wrote that you want to travel to marvelous places, climb Mount Everest, or help the poor. But can you achieve similar goals and have similar experiences with the resources available to you right now?

An ancient Greek philosopher, Epicurus (341–270 B.C.E.), held that the good life and happiness were found by pursuing pleasure and avoiding pain. Sounds like common sense—but Epicurus would have told us that we're doing it all wrong.

The key to a pleasurable existence, according to Epicurus, is to have a peaceful and simple life, with friends. When we think of hedonism—living life for nothing but pleasure—we tend to think of a much more complicated kind of life. Rare and hard-to-obtain pleasures may be great, but think of everything you have to sacrifice to get them! With great wealth there are opportunities to enjoy great luxury, or to enjoy being a great benefactor, but we soon develop expensive tastes. Once our happiness is bound up in becoming and remaining wealthy, fear and uncertainty begin to dominate our lives. Life becomes more and more about securing the resources that we've made our happiness depend on, and less about doing things that actually make us happy.

To be happy and peaceful, Epicurus advocated living simply, and not getting too involved in wealth, politics, or even physical desires like those for sex or food. As often happens, his doctrine has become twisted over time, and today "Epicurean" refers to a taste for very sophisticated and refined foods. For a true sense of Epicurus's view of the good life, cook a simple thick soup of water, lentils, turnips, and some salt. Eat it with crusty bread and butter in the company of a friend, and then go for a walk together. Try it, and then ask yourself what else you've made harder than it needs to be.

Aristotle's Altruism

Was there a time recently when you went out of your way to do something nice for someone else? What did you do?

_____

_____

_____

_____

Were you glad you did? Why or why not?

_____

_____

_____

What about a time when you put your own interests ahead of others—was it worth it? What made it so—or if it wasn't, why not?

_____

_____

_____

_____

The Philosophy

Common sense would tell you that doing something for yourself should make you happy. It seems like a no-brainer. But it's more complicated than it might seem.

Happiness is a confusing, fleeting thing. The ancient Greek philosopher Aristotle (384–322 B.C.E.) was a pupil of Plato (429–347 B.C.E.), who eventually broke from the ideas of his mentor. He held that happiness was a matter of realizing human potential. When we do the right thing, we are following higher, distinctively human parts of ourselves, like reason, character, and virtue. When we act out of self-interest, we follow lower parts of ourselves that we have in common with other living things: pride, anger, desire, and simple hunger. According to Aristotle, someone who is purely self-interested can never be happy; only through virtuous action can we be happy.

That's why when we do something out of self-interest, we often feel guilty or ashamed, and when we act altruistically and purely out of a concern for others, we feel good about ourselves. Happiness can only be reached indirectly; you end up happiest when you just try to do the right thing, and when you try to make yourself happy, you often enough end up feeling worse.

Aristotle was a harsh realist, though. Goods of fortune, like wealth and health, can't make us happy, but their absence can prevent us from becoming happy, or even virtuous. How can you cultivate care and generosity when you have no resources? How can you learn temperance and how to moderate your desires, if you are always living paycheck to paycheck? Putting self-interest first might be worth it if you're struggling just to get by. The problem is that once we start out this way, we develop selfish habits; we end up with goods of fortune, but little virtue.

Here Comes Honey Boo Boo
and John Stuart Mill

What's one of your guilty pleasures—a "bad" television program, secret romance novel habit, or something similar?

_____

_____

If you feel guilty about it, why do you keep doing it?

_____

_____

On the other hand, if it's something you enjoy, and it's not immoral, why do you feel guilty about it to begin with?

_____

_____

Everyone has guilty pleasures. What if we made them central to our lives instead of hiding them away? It's hard to imagine. What would change? Would our world be a better place, or a worse one?

_____

_____

_____

_____

The Philosophy

John Stuart Mill (1806–1873), a British utilitarian and political philosopher, thought that the right action was always the one that provided the greatest good for the greatest number. But how do you figure out what is good for someone—or for anyone?

Mill said, first, that the only proof that something is worth valuing is that people, in fact, value it. By giving up on the idea that we should adopt some single conception of "the good life," he was able to talk about how we ought to help as many people to be happy as we can, but without telling them *how* to be happy! But what about gluttons, scoundrels, and cretins? Can their "happiness" really be considered equal to the happiness of a decent person of refined taste who cares for others?

To fix the problem, Mill added a criterion to what counts as part of happiness. Not everyone is able to appreciate a quiet evening spent with a good book, but those who can tend to prefer it to watching trashy TV. That means that watching trashy TV is actually a lesser happiness, even though there may be many who can't really appreciate a good book, and who *think* that trashy TV makes them happy.

As Mill put it in *Utilitarianism*: "It is better to be a human being dissatisfied than a pig satisfied; better to be Socrates dissatisfied than a fool satisfied. And if the fool, or the pig, are of a different opinion, it is because they only know their own side of the question. The other party to the comparison knows both sides."

The Stoic's Freedom

We usually regard freedom and self-determination to be central to a good life. When have you sacrificed something else in your life—perhaps in your work life, love life, or just your way of life—to ensure that you are able to make your own choices and not be dependent on others?

_____

_____

_____

_____

Was this sacrifice worth it? Why?

_____

_____

_____

_____

If not, why not? If so, how much further would you go?

_____

_____

_____

_____

The Philosophy

On the previous page, you were asked to look at what your personal freedom meant to you, and what comforts or happiness you'd give up to keep it. Most people would probably make sacrifices to be independent, *to a certain extent*. But there are certain things that just aren't worth it, right?

Not according to Stoicism, a philosophy very popular in ancient Rome. It taught that the key to a good life was to identify what was *up to us*, and what was not, and to care *only* about those things that were up to us. Epictetus (55–135), a Stoic philosopher and freed slave, outlined the meaning and implications of this simple idea in his *Enchiridion* (Handbook), which was a kind of ancient self-help book.

To remain free and in control of our own happiness, we must care only about things that are up to us. "So, you want to compete in the Olympic games?" Epictetus asks. 'If you say you wish to train hard, push yourself constantly, twist your ankle, eat sand, and, in the end, lose—then you may compete and be free and in control! But if you want to *win*, you are a fool, for this is not up to you, and this desire puts others in control of whether you are able to reach your goals and be happy.'

Your body also isn't up to you; others can make choices about it. There's a story that when Epictetus was still a slave, his master, enraged about some perceived wrong, broke Epictetus's leg. Epictetus did not resist: He knew what happened to his body was not up to him and that caring about it would only deliver control of his life into the hands of others. By deciding not to care for his physical welfare, Epictetus remained entirely free and in control even as he was in chains.

Do you have what it takes to be free? Is it worth it?

The Nietzschean Marathon

Is happiness really what you're aiming for in life? Most of us would say yes, and yet every day we make decisions that actually make our lives harder in the day-to-day reality of living, for example, training for a marathon, or taking the hardest classes in school.

Make a short list of the things you've chosen to do in life and to care about that have increased the suffering, struggle, and trials in your life.

1. _____

2. _____

3. _____

4. _____

5. _____

For what reason or reasons did you make these choices?

_____

_____

_____

_____

_____

_____

_____

The Philosophy

Did you say "Because I will be happier in the end, having gone through these struggles"? If that's the case, why don't you decide to eat an entire airplane? Now that's *really* difficult, so it should make you *really* happy, right?

Go back and look at those questions again. I'll wait here.

Okay, you're back. Have you got another answer, or several of them? The point here is that while today we have fallen into the habit of acting like everything we do is in the service of happiness, we actually care about plenty of other things as well.

In his book *Thus Spake Zarathustra*, German philosopher Friedrich Nietzsche (1844–1900) gives us a vision of the tragic dissipation of humanity: The Last Man. The Last Man seeks only happiness, and is free from the toil and turmoil of questioning and striving and seeking. But it is not too late, Nietzsche tells us through his character Zarathustra: We still have enough chaos within us to give birth to a dancing star!

Every so often, a new study comes out on parenting and happiness, and most often these studies find that having kids makes us feel less self-satisfaction and less happiness on a day-to-day basis. When confronted with this empirical data, parents usually insist, "It'll be worth it!" and "I'll be happier in the end!" Why not just recognize that happiness isn't the only reason we do things, and certainly isn't the only reason things are worth doing? How empty and worthless the world would be if our own private enjoyment were the only reason to get up in the morning!

Sisyphus's Toil

What goals do you have in life? Think about family, career, hobbies, and personal passions.

1. _____
2. _____
3. _____
4. _____
5. _____

What will they amount to when you're done? What difference will they have made?

1. _____
2. _____
3. _____
4. _____
5. _____

What difference will they have made to the world after you have passed away and a couple more generations have lived and died?

1. _____
2. _____
3. _____
4. _____
5. _____

The Philosophy

Are you depressed yet? Well, it'll get worse before it gets better.

French-Algerian absurdist philosopher Albert Camus (1913–1960) adapted an ancient Greek story—the myth of Sisyphus—to force us to confront the meaninglessness of life. Imagine Sisyphus, punished eternally to push a rock up a hill, only to watch it roll down the other side every time. A more meaningless eternity cannot be imagined. Camus asks us how this is different from our lives. We all struggle and toil to achieve our goals, and whatever we put together is taken apart in time. What we do for ourselves is taken apart by death, but even what we do for others —to care for the sick, help the needy, or advance science and human understanding— is erased from the earth by time and death. As the Book of Ecclesiastes puts it, "All is vanity and a striving after wind."

Camus asks us, though, "Can we imagine Sisyphus happy?" Camus thinks we can. We can imagine Sisyphus's pleasure in the wind as he descends the hill, the enjoyment of work and of the body as he puts his shoulder to the rock once more. And so too he tells us that just because life amounts to nothing does not mean it isn't worth living.

Richard Taylor (1919–2003), an American philosopher, asks us further: What if Sisyphus desired nothing more than to push this rock endlessly? Then he might find not just moments of happiness in his toil; he might find the whole process, devoid of an outcome as it may be, to be *meaningful*. What is it to find something meaningful other than to desire to do it? Is this closer to what our lives are like: meaningless in that they amount to little or nothing, but meaningful to us through the process of living itself?

The Device Paradigm

Even if we find our lives to be meaningful, that certainly doesn't apply to every part of them. What are some of the most meaningless things you're going to have to do today?

1. _____

2. _____

3. _____

4. _____

5. _____

What purposes do those activities play in your life? Are there more meaningful things you could be doing to serve those purposes instead? For example, could you go for a run through the woods or on the beach instead of putting in time on the treadmill at the gym? Could you make a family meal instead of picking up something on the way home and eating a rushed meal in front of the television?

_____

_____

_____

_____

_____

_____

The Philosophy

Meaninglessness isn't just an abstract concern tied to death and purpose; we struggle with meaninglessness and tedium on a daily basis. Some things need to get done, but if we do everything just to finish it and sacrifice taking actions and completing tasks in a rich and fulfilling way, then we're left with a life where we've sacrificed the meaningful stuff so that we can do more and more empty and inane things more quickly!

Contemporary American philosopher Albert Borgmann (1937–) thinks part of this trend has to do with our technological worldview. The need for warmth, for example, once structured our lives and our families. The hearth was a focal point in the home; its fire gave each family member a role to play: gathering and chopping wood; building the fire in the morning; cooking on the woodstove. The centralized heat source in the house brought and kept the family together throughout the day's activities. Today, on the other hand, with devices like central heat and gas or electric stoves, warmth is provided through a simple switch, and the family is no longer structured by these roles. Each family member no longer need contribute to the shared process—nor do they communally share its benefits. The family is not brought together into a central room; instead each retreats to his or her own separate space. Along with the disappearance of the hearth, the family disintegrates.

Now, technology is clearly a good thing in many ways, but the things we tend to find meaningful depart from the technological drive toward efficiency. We go for a walk after dinner, and we say "This is nice. Why don't we do this more often?" And yet, we don't. Actions taken in slower, usually more complicated ways are often the things we find meaningful, yet for the sake of convenience, we choose efficiency. Resist it! Cook a nice meal instead of going through a drive-through! Grow a garden, even though you could just buy vegetables in the supermarket! Make some music (even if it's awful) instead of just listening to it!

Marx's Alienation

In your work life, how much can you choose what you do, or how you do it? Could work life be structured to give you more freedom?

_____

_____

_____

_____

_____

What difference does the work you do make in the lives of others? What control do you have over the meaning and impact of your work? If you work for a corporation, how much do you control the meaning and impact of your company?

_____

_____

_____

_____

_____

_____

_____

The Philosophy

You're almost certainly familiar with Karl Marx's (1818–1883) opposition to capitalism, but the German philosopher's reasoning is less well-known. It can offer insights to all of us living under capitalism, whether or not we wish to see the system end.

Marx believed that what made humans distinct from other animals was our ability to change the world based on our own desires and creative vision. This ability to not just consume, but to also change and create the world, is what he called our *species-being*. In his early, more humanistic and less economic work, he outlined several ways in which those of us who must work to survive are alienated from our basic nature—from our species-being. We are alienated in that we produce objects not of our design or choice; we produce them using tools and techniques that are not our own; we use materials that are not ours; and the value of our labor, crystallized in the products we manufacture, belongs to someone else. We do not have ownership over the product of our labor, and during our working hours we do not have ownership over ourselves.

We sell the most human part of our lives—our creative, productive abilities—which becomes "labor"; a necessity and a burden. We then feel free only outside of working hours, where we concentrate on our lesser, animal needs for consumption and rest. In this way, the worker is alienated from her own humanity; she is least herself when building and creating, and feels most at home when she is least human.

The argument was much more striking before the labor movement, motivated in part by Marx's arguments, brought about the eight-hour workday and the weekend, and abolished child labor. But even today, many workers feel this alienation keenly. If you don't you're one of the lucky few.

Marcuse and the Rat Race

Assuming you're working full-time, about 35 percent of your waking life during your working years will be spent at work. Are you happy to have your work achievements take up over a third of your life for these years? Why or why not?

_____

_____

_____

_____

_____

_____

Consider how many other people are similarly devoting this portion of their lives to work, and what it all adds up to. Is our standard of living worth a third of our lives? Is this what a third of humanity's hours should amount to?

_____

_____

_____

_____

_____

The Philosophy

Just as it's said that no one wishes on her deathbed that she had spent more time at the office, so too we might imagine that if we could look back from the end of human history, we wouldn't wish we had spent more time working. Instead, we tend to think that knowledge, understanding, discovery, togetherness, connection, creativity, art, and beauty make up the meaning of our species, if anything does.

And yet, as German-Jewish philosopher Herbert Marcuse (1898–1979) pointed out, once we achieved the forty-hour work week, we did not struggle further for the thirty- or twenty-hour work week. Once we shifted from working in order to free everyone from sickness and hunger to working in order to make things quicker-faster-better, we failed to slow down enough to live. What sacrifices have we made as a people to have faster mobile phones, tougher plastics, and hundreds of television channels? What would our lives be like if we had just spent less time working? What other forms of richness would we have instead?

I find this question especially important in the light of our current dialogue about "job creation." We have no shortage of wealth, food, and shelter—we only have trouble making up things for people to do to earn the resources that we already have. Why not make thirty hours the standard for full-time, benefits-earning employment? It's complicated, of course, and we'll talk more about it in Chapter 5: Economic Justice, but we should at least talk about having more people do less, to include everyone in the prosperity of our society, while simultaneously allowing everyone more time to do the things that they find meaningful.

Embodied Values

Reflect back on the things you've talked about throughout this chapter on happiness and the meaning of life. The things you desire, that make you happy, or that you find meaningful—how did you come to hold those values?

_____

_____

_____

_____

_____

Think about how you live your life. Do you embody values, both for happiness and for a meaningful life, that you would hold up to others as an example of a life well lived? If so, how so; if not, what's something you could change?

_____

_____

_____

_____

_____

The Philosophy

We don't enter the world with a predetermined set of values; we learn them through our life experiences. Most of all, we learn them through our experiences with others. Did you identify any particular people who have served as models or instructors in a life well lived?

French existentialist Jean-Paul Sartre (1905–1980) held that one of the most significant elements of belief in atheism was that, if there is no God, then we are on our own to determine what our lives are to be about—and that this means that in deciding for ourselves, we also decide for all humanity, because there is no authority on and determiner of what life is about except for various people making their own choices. The same sort of thing can be said from a religious perspective: Even those who decide to listen to one religious authority or another, or follow one text or another, make that decision in a world that is underdetermining, in which we all muddle through using one another as examples.

When you decide how to live, you implicitly claim that your kind of life is a kind of life worth living. You claim that your goals are important enough to expend the hours we walk upon the earth pursuing. We do not receive our values; we choose them, even when we happen to choose to believe the things we are brought up believing.

Would you be happy to have the values embodied in your life be the values of humanity? In Sartre's view, there is no source of values other than people's choosing, and so we have not only the freedom to do whatever we wish, but the responsibility to choose on behalf of all others as well.

CHAPTER 2

God

The history of European philosophy is tightly bound with the history of Christian theology, so there's an emphasis here on Christian views. I've tried to present things so that these questions and ideas are as valuable as possible for those of you who are not Christians, but some of the issues don't translate well to other views. If you're Jewish or Muslim, most of the issues will apply equally for you; if you're Hindu or Buddhist, it'll be hit-and-miss; if you're agnostic or atheist, well, you'll probably just be playing along. But that's valuable too—valuable to better understand what it's like to have faith, and to enjoy the intricacies and subtleties of religious reasoning. I'm not a Christian, and I have a kind of pure enjoyment of St. Thomas Aquinas's writing; pure because I don't have faith in his sources, and have little concern for his topics or answers—and yet nonetheless I enjoy and appreciate the grace and wisdom of his discussion itself.

It might be good to remind you before you start in here that philosophy is about hard-nosed analysis and criticism. Philosophy is not interested in being reassuring, and it is not interested in making you comfortable. It's interested in discovering the truth, and that means being open to the possibility that the truth is horrible.

Why Is There Something Rather Than Nothing?

No, seriously: Why is there something rather than nothing?

_____

_____

_____

Things are happening right now, caused by things that just happened just before the things happening now. And those things must have been caused by something before them, and so on. Doesn't there have to be some kind of first cause, that isn't itself caused? Or is it possible that there is no beginning?

_____

_____

_____

If there is a first cause, mustn't it have its own will and ability to choose? If not, wouldn't it have to have been caused by something else to start everything into motion? But if that's the case, then we haven't reached the first cause yet, have we?

_____

_____

_____

_____

The Philosophy

Ok, yes, these are leading questions. You can see where this is going. These questions are the basis for what's called the cosmological proof of God's existence.

It's an argument that's been given by many different philosophers, including Aristotle and René Descartes (1596–1650), but this is the basic form. Where did all this stuff come from? How did the chain of cause and effect get started? Change and matter need to come from somewhere. And, in particular, it's unsatisfying to just say that everything's always been around and been in motion, since, well, how can there be an infinite series of effects without some cause to start everything off? Unless you say that there is some kind of "unmoved mover" to get things going, we just have to throw up our hands. Even the "Big Bang" theory doesn't resolve the issue. Why did it "bang"? Where did the thing that "banged" come from?

Still, this doesn't really prove God's existence, although plenty of philosophers wrongly thought it did. Sure, we can't explain the universe otherwise, but should we really expect to be able to understand the origin of the universe, or to be so sure that just because human reason says there must be a beginning that it must be so in actuality? Even the answer that "God did it" just puts off the cosmological question: We might ask, then, where God came from? If we assert that God is *sui generis*—that He made Himself by Himself—that's really just as uninformative as saying that the universe made itself by itself.

The bottom line here is that, whatever we believe, we should have humility about it. Because whatever we believe, it doesn't really answer the question, and it sure seems like nothing ever will.

The Divine Watchmaker

Pick up a stone and look at it for a minute. Where did that stone come from? Could it have come from a series of purposeless natural forces? Or must there have been something directing its creation?

_____

_____

_____

_____

Imagine, instead, picking up a watch. Could it have come from a series of purposeless natural forces?

_____

_____

_____

Consider the diversity and intricate interconnection of all the elements of nature—plants and animals, earth and atmosphere. Is it not more like a watch than a stone? Could nature have come from a series of purposeless natural forces?

_____

_____

_____

The Philosophy

Again, these are leading questions. In this case, they are the questions asked by English philosopher William Paley (1743–1805), in his famous "watchmaker analogy." The analogy is a kind of *teleological* argument for God's existence—"teleological" in that it is an argument based on the idea of a purpose (from the Greek *telos*).

The watch appears *designed* to work, and this implies a *designer*. Nature, for it's part, resembles a watch in its intricacy and precision, and this seems to imply a designer as well. Contemporary versions of this argument call attention to the complexity of, for example, the eye, and ask how intermediary forms could be evolutionarily adaptive—and, if they are not adaptive, why would they have come about unless it's part of a larger plan? These arguments call into question the idea that natural selection alone could account for the origin of human and animal bodies.

It's interesting to see what this argument does and does not establish. These argu-ments for "intelligent design" theories are often used to argue for a Christian concep-tion of creation, but they are just as compat-ible with any kind of intelligent designer—a flying spaghetti monster, for example. The teleological argument also doesn't establish that evolutionary biology and other sciences won't explain the complexity of design, given time. After all, most theists believe that God works mostly through natural proc-esses rather than miracles, so God's design could quite possibly be realized through sci-entifically describable natural forces.

But is science able to explain *every-thing*? Maybe. Maybe not. We're a long way from finding out. But whether or not you believe in a Designer, you're better off not using it as an explanation for anything. To say "God did it" only halts inquiry into nature, where we might be able to figure out how things happened—and that's at least as interesting if you think that this scientif-ically discoverable natural history is also an expression of God's will.

The Problem of Evil

If God exists, is God entirely good, or partially good and partially evil? How can you tell?

_____

_____

_____

_____

If God is entirely good, where does the evil in the world come from? Did God create it? How could evil come from an entirely good being?

_____

_____

_____

If God did not create the evil in the world, why does God allow it to exist?

_____

_____

_____

_____

THE PHILOSOPHER'S BOOK OF QUESTIONS & ANSWERS

The Philosophy

This is what's called "The Problem of Evil," and it presents some serious problems to a traditional Judeo-Christian notion of God. There are several possible responses that depart from this notion of God:

* God doesn't exist.
* God exists, but is partially evil.
* God is good, but not omnipotent, and so evil creeps into the world despite God's goodness and love.
* There is a good divine force, but an evil one as well, strong enough to compete with God's will, and our world is a battleground between them.

There are also several ways that Christian philosophers have responded to the problem of evil in other ways without departing from a traditional Judeo-Christian understanding of God. Most famous is the "free-will defense": Evil enters the world through human choice, and free will is so important to God that He allows evil for its sake. (We'll talk more about that argument in Chapter 7: Aspects of the Self.) Another interesting response is to simply deny that evil exists.

St. Augustine (354–430), a North African philosopher, claimed that what we call evil is simply the absence of good, just like darkness is not a real thing, but only the absence of light. He asked what happens to a physical wound or sickness when we are healed. Does it flutter away from your body to a new host? Of course not; it simply disappears, showing that the injury was not a real thing, but only an absence of health. In the same way, evil is not real, it is only the absence of good. We fall into evil and suffering because God made us from nothing, and when we move away from God's goodness, we tend to return to nothing.

The Value of Suffering

What great trials have you faced in life? Have they changed you for the better or for the worse? If you don't think you've faced any great trials, think about someone who has, and imagine her or his answer.

_____

_____

_____

_____

What are some examples of kinds of suffering that almost always improve the people who undergo them?

_____

_____

_____

_____

What kinds of suffering are unlikely to improve those who undergo them? Is there such a thing as a pure loss—suffering unredeemed or unredeemable by growth and progress?

_____

_____

_____

_____

The Philosophy

Another possible response to the problem of evil—called a *theodicy* or justification of God—is to claim that God allows evil because suffering is necessary for human development. Without the negative, we cannot appreciate the positive, and some elements of human greatness can only be achieved through suffering, strife, and loss.

Many have put forth versions of this theodicy; among the earliest was St. Irenaeus (d. 202), and among the most famous, the German philosopher Gottfried Leibniz (1646–1716). The basic idea is that even though there is evil and suffering, this is still the best of all possible worlds, either because the evil in the world is outweighed by the good that is made possible through that evil, or because it is not logically possible for God to have created a world without these flaws—for example, to have created beings who are not, through their finite nature, subject to errors in knowledge and moral failings.

Others have argued against this view. For example, the German philosopher Arthur Schopenhauer (1788–1860) argued that you could see immediately that the good in the world does not always outweigh the evil simply by comparing "the respective feelings of two animals, one of which is engaged in eating the other." Surely the pleasures of the table are not so great! William R. Jones (1933–2012) put forth a fascinating challenge to this theodicy in his 1973 book, *Is God a White Racist?* Can we assert that "the harder the cross, the brighter the crown"—can we maintain that suffering will be redeemed by God—in the face of a history of racially discriminatory violence and suffering?

What justification can be given for God's inaction in the face of the enslavement of black people, or in the face of the attempted genocide of the Jews? Is the very idea that such horrors could be justified an insult to those who have suffered and died?

Punishment and Redemption

For a moment at least, adopt the idea that suffering is sometimes a divine punishment for sin. Can this explain the suffering of terminally ill infants and children or of an animal burned alive in a forest fire? What other explanation can you offer?

_____

_____

_____

_____

How should we differentiate deserved from undeserved punishment in the suffering of others?

_____

_____

_____

_____

How should we separate deserved from undeserved punishment in our own suffering?

_____

_____

_____

The Philosophy

The suffering of innocent individuals, like the suffering of peoples and races, provides a difficult challenge to any theodicy. This is one among many philosophical themes explored in *The Plague*, a Nobel Prize–winning novel by the French-Algerian absurdist philosopher Albert Camus (1913–1960).

In the story, an Algerian town suffers a rare outbreak of bubonic plague, which kills much of the population before the town's doctors are able to develop a cure. Father Paneloux, a Jesuit priest, gives a sermon early on in the epidemic, in which he calls forth the image of a threshing floor: It is through the violence of the plague, he claims, that God separates the wheat from the chaff.

After watching a child suffer a slow and painful death, Paneloux finds that he can no longer believe that suffering can always be justified as a punishment or a trial. He asks himself instead whether the suffering of an innocent can be made up for by the eternal bliss of heaven. But if this is so, then Jesus's suffering on the cross becomes meaningless, because it is only a moment of pain outweighed by an eternity of happiness. Jesus's suffering cannot serve as a means of human redemption if it is not truly a sacrifice. Paneloux finds he can't brush away the suffering of a child by asserting that all will be made right in the next world. Instead, "he, Father Paneloux, would keep faith with that great symbol of all suffering, the tortured body on the Cross; he would stand fast, his back to the wall, and face honestly the terrible problem of a child's agony."

Faith and Evidence

Do you think God exists, and why? What evidence do you have in favor of your position? How did you come by this evidence?

_____

_____

_____

_____

Do you consider this evidence to be conclusive, and your position to be beyond doubt? If so, why do you think others remain unconvinced?

_____

_____

_____

If you don't consider your position to be beyond doubt, what kind of evidence would move you to reconsider your position?

_____

_____

_____

The Philosophy

Most (
ion a
and (
usual
expe
evide
able
ever
we t
wha

Am(
191
thir
in
exa
like
sta
les
an
ab
be

...you can't really be certain of it, you will be ...iendly and outgoing, and your belief ...d to make it true.

...a slightly different example, if you are ...ering marrying, but are not sure that ...ouse will live up to your hopes, your ...will poison and end the relationship— ...through *believing* in her goodness are ...le to have a life together in which you ...le to *find out* whether she is the won- ...woman you believe her to be.

...eligious faith, according to James, ...the same way. Belief in the goodness ...world tends to make the world good, ...belief in religion opens us up to the ...of experiences that justify faith, which ...doubter may never experience. This ...n't mean that we all necessarily *ought* ...ve religious faith or that faith is correct, ...James claims we have a *right* to choose ...elieve, even in the absence of sufficient ...ence.

The Euthyphro Dilemma

Think of a religious text that you believe expresses the will of God (or imagine for the moment that you believe there is such a thing). Why is God telling you how you should act?

_____

_____

_____

_____

_____

_____

If that text told you to do something you believe to be immoral, would you do it?

_____

_____

_____

_____

_____

_____

The Philosophy

You probably found the second question frustrating. Very likely, you found the premise behind the question impossible. If God is good, how could God tell you to do something immoral? Or, alternately, if God tells you to do it, doesn't that *make* it the right thing to do?

This is what's called "The Euthyphro Dilemma," named for Plato's dialogue "The Euthyphro." In the dialogue, Socrates (469–399 B.C.E.) confronts an earnest man named Euthyphro about his beliefs about piety. Piety, in Euthyphro's view, is doing what the gods love. But why, asks Socrates, do the gods love some things rather than others? Because those things are holy, answers Euthyphro. This brings up several troubling questions:

* If it is pious to do what the gods love, and the gods love what is holy, then why not just say that it's pious to do what is holy, and leave the gods out of the whole discussion?

* Alternately, if it isn't holiness that makes the pious action pious, then couldn't the gods love what is unholy— and wouldn't that, then, be what is pious?

In the context of modern Christianity, the question is whether good and evil are based on God's will, or whether God's will is based on good and evil. Either position appears heretical. If good means nothing but "what God says to do" and evil means nothing but "what God says not to do"—this is called divine command theory—then God could say that murder is right, and it would be . . . and that sure doesn't seem right. And worse yet, how can we claim that God is good, if "good" just means "whatever God says"? On the other hand, if God is telling us to do what is good because God is good, then good and evil exist independently of God, and God is just offering advice about a moral system that God is Himself subject to!

Natural Law

Think again about a text that you believe contains the will of God—or, again, imagine that you believe there is such a thing. Can someone who doesn't accept that text be moral? Why or why not?

_____

_____

_____

_____

_____

_____

That text undoubtedly has a history, and a cultural origin. Could a just God judge those who never had a chance to read that text? In a Christian context, how can God judge those who lived before the birth of Jesus?

_____

_____

_____

_____

_____

The Philosophy

In many faiths, this isn't such a big issue. In Hinduism and Buddhism, for example, you can be a good person without any particular knowledge about this or that deity. You just have to be compassionate, care for others, stand for what's right, and so on. We can all pretty well figure out that stuff on our own, even though moral and religious texts might be helpful along the way. This has, however, been a big issue in the Christian tradition, where some theologians have claimed that "Revealed Law"—the word of God, contained in the Bible, and sent to guide humanity —is necessary for salvation. It seems a bit unfair to others, though, and the question of the "righteous heathens," like the good and moral people born before Jesus, has been an issue of debate.

One way of mitigating this seeming divine injustice is the idea of "Natural Law." The idea is that God's will can be determined by looking to God's creation, where we can see *implicitly* the rules for moral conduct that are stated *explicitly* in God's word. Through use of reason alone, we can determine, for example, that we ought to treat others just as we would like others to treat us. Whatever you might think about the idea of Natural Law, it is certainly striking that every culture and religion seems to have its own version of the Golden Rule.

On this view, even our bodies can instruct us in God's will through Natural Law. For example, philosopher and Doctor of the Church St. Thomas Aquinas (1225–1274), argued in *On Kingship* that we could tell that God intended us to live in community with one another and under a government because He created us without tough hides or sharp claws. It's a bit undignified, but effective: We learn to live along with others, to be citizens and subjects, because our other choice is to die cold and alone or fall prey to wild beasts.

Bodily Urges

Based on this idea of Natural Law, why might it be that other bodily attributes sometimes seem to drive us toward less moral behavior? Why would God make us this way?

_____

_____

_____

_____

_____

_____

Do you consider any of your bodily urges immoral? If not, why do you think others might? If so, what do you do to control these urges?

_____

_____

_____

_____

_____

_____

THE PHILOSOPHER'S BOOK OF QUESTIONS & ANSWERS

The Philosophy

For creatures said to be created in the image of God, we are awfully messy, hairy, smelly, and desirous things, aren't we? If this idea of Natural Law is going to hold up, we need to have some explanation for why, if nature is supposed to be a guide to the same moral law contained in Revealed Law, our bodily natures seem to drive us into all kinds of coveting and licentiousness.

Both Augustine and Aquinas were influenced by Aristotle's understanding of the human as a "rational animal." In this view, we are animals first and rationality, the soul, in the Christian sense, is added later. (This is why, until the nineteenth century, the Church regarded abortion as morally acceptable—through the first trimester, the fetus was thought to be just an animal, with no soul.) So, we have our animal nature as well as our higher nature, and that means that we retain some biological imperatives and urges proper to animals, as well as those distinctively proper to humans. The pleasure we take in the body is natural and proper to our animal nature, and contributes to its well-being. The pleasures of the table drive us to maintain our bodily health, which we need for our individual survival, and sexual pleasure drives us to procreate, which we need for the continuation of humanity. Our nature, though, should also teach us that reason, which humans alone have, is more important than the body, which we have in common with all animals, and so we should see (as did Aristotle and Plato) that it is right that our desires be kept in check rather than given free rein. But those urges are not sinful in themselves—they are proper to our animal nature. The sin comes through acting like mere animals.

In a particularly awkward passage, Chapter 17 of his *City of God*, Augustine even discusses erections. He claims that this involuntary and sometimes unwelcome response of the human body "testifies against the disobedience of man" in the Garden of Eden. So there you go.

Today's "Abrahams"

What if you began hearing a voice that told you to do things? Terrible things. What if it said it was God? Would you follow the voice?

_____

_____

_____

_____

What if it really was God, and you knew that with certainty, somehow? Would you follow its instructions?

_____

_____

_____

What if someone else had this experience? What would it take to convince you to help him to commit the atrocities that he says God has told him to do?

_____

_____

_____

_____

The Philosophy

Of course, we don't even want to consider such a thing, but the Danish philosopher Søren Kierkegaard (1813–1855) said that no Christian can avoid these questions (and we can add, neither can any Jew or Muslim).

In the story of Abraham, God tells Abraham to kill his son Isaac, who is Abraham's greatest love and pride, and who has done nothing to deserve this fate. No moral justification is given—Isaac is to be a ritual sacrifice to God, murdered by the command of the same God who commanded us not to murder. This shows us, according to Kierkegaard, that faith lies beyond the realm of the ethical. Faith can demand things that cannot be explained or justified.

Should the priest, hearing a parishioner speak of hearing such a divine command, dismiss this as insanity? Can he, while remaining a Christian? Would this not condemn Abraham as well? Shouldn't the priest, instead, walk with his parishioner, as he would have walked with Abraham and Isaac to Mount Moriah? How can any answer here be acceptable?

It is a question that is all the more pressing today, in the light of religious terrorism—not just Islamist attacks, but abortion clinic shootings, the Atlanta Olympic bombing, and "collateral damage" of innumerable Muslim children in the Middle East. Anyone in the Judeo-Christian tradition cannot ignore the story of Abraham—or that of Samson, a biblical "suicide bomber" who brought about his own death in order to wreak vengeance upon the Philistines (Judges 16:30)—and this requires some difficult thought.

CHAPTER 3

Morals

How ought we to act? On what basis do we decide on courses of action? What do we mean when we say something is "right" or "wrong" in a moral sense? These are among the many questions that we will most definitely not answer by the end of this chapter. We'll take a pretty good look at things, though, taking a quick trip through deontology, utilitarianism, virtue ethics, ethics of care, and a couple of issues in religious morality.

Questions in ethical theory, for the most part, aren't about particular situations. For the most part, they have less to do with *what* to believe about right and wrong than they do with *why* we believe what we believe. Any decent ethical theory will recognize the complexity of our lives, and will give us troubling or ambiguous answers to questions about how to act in troubling or ambiguous circumstances. And yet, at the same time, such cases help to throw into sharp contrast the differences between one theory and another. As a result, we end up looking at some pretty inventive and extreme examples. Sometimes these "thought experiments" help us to clarify our views—but sometimes they make complex issues seem far too simple. You'll see what I mean.

By the way, most philosophers use the words "ethics" and "morality" interchangeably. (Some do draw a distinction, but those distinctions are pretty idiosyncratic to those particular philosophers.) To keep things clear, I'll be using the two terms as entirely synonymous.

The Best of Intentions

Can good people do bad things? Give some examples.

_____

_____

_____

_____

When good people do things that turn out badly, or have unintended harmful results, does this make them less good or less moral? Why?

_____

_____

_____

_____

Regardless of what it says about the person's morality, can an action be a bad action if it is done with good intentions? Or is any action taken with good intentions a good action?

_____

_____

_____

_____

_____

The Philosophy

Bad people can clearly do bad things, and an action taken with the intent to harm clearly says something bad about the person with that intention. But are the best of intentions always enough?

Immanuel Kant (1724–1804) thought morality was entirely about our intentions. It makes sense that someone as religious as Kant would believe so—this means that we are entirely in control of whether we act morally or immorally, and that helps to justify the idea that God will reward or punish us according to our moral worth. However, Kant's argument for the idea has nothing to do with his faith. He argues instead that having a good will toward others is the only truly and purely good thing that we *can* have, and whether you are a good person comes down to whether you have a good will. Even virtues like cleverness and con-

viction can become evil when held by those with bad intentions.

But surely those who commit evil acts often do so because they have "good intentions." Anders Breivik, for example, explained his mass murders in Norway in 2011 as a way to raise awareness of the "dangers" of multiculturalism and feminism. Thankfully, Kant gave us an objective test for whether our intentions really are good. He called this the "categorical imperative": Always act according to intentions that could be adopted by everyone else as well, and which, if adopted by everybody, would result in a world that we'd like to live in. So Breivik is clearly out: The intention to murder, for whatever reason, if universalized, would eventually result in us all being dead. And, for that matter, intolerance of other cultures and the subjection of women don't work out either.

The White Lie

Have you ever told a white lie? Of course you have. Describe a lie or half-truth that you've told that you think was clearly justifiable.

_____

_____

_____

_____

What good outcomes did you close off by lying? What could the truth have changed, if things had gone well?

_____

_____

_____

What kinds of circumstances or conditions do you think justify lies? What needs to be at stake in order to justify a lie—or, alternately, how trivial does something have to be before you are justified in lying about it?

_____

_____

_____

_____

The Philosophy

As we saw before, just telling yourself or believing that you have good intentions, for Kant, isn't enough. You still have bad intentions in reality if, for example, your so-called "good intentions" are "to save the white race from losing its dominance over others." But Kant's categorical imperative also doesn't give you a free pass on a bad action if your eventual goal is good—say, if Breivik's goal had been peace, love, and understanding, Kant would condemn killing as a means to that end as well. This means, for Kant, some things are just wrong no matter what, and while that might make intuitive sense when we're talking about killing people, it also means that an injustice is wrong even when it serves the greater good, that breaking the law is wrong even if it's a bad law, and that there's no such thing as a "white lie."

Many have taken this to be a fatal flaw in Kant's theory, but a pretty good defense of it can actually be put together. Here's a troubling example that Kant himself took on:

Imagine that someone comes to your door intending to murder your friend, who is hiding in your house. Lying is wrong for Kant, because it can't be universalized: If everybody deceived others when it was helpful, deception would become impossible, because no one would believe anyone. So you can't lie to the murderer at the door—which seems crazy. But consider: You can still defend your friend, and by being honest with the man at the door, you show him respect as a person still able to choose to do the right thing. Deception treats him as a mere murderer; honesty confronts him with the truth and gives him the chance to redeem himself. Always telling the truth may be hard, and sometimes dangerous, but no one ever said being moral was always easy or safe.

Truth or Consequences

Imagine you answer an ad on Craigslist for someone who wants you to be executor of his will. He says he doesn't trust his family to do it. When he dies and you open the folder, you understand why: His entire estate is to be given to a neo-Nazi group. Would you be justified in "misplacing" the will in a nearby fireplace?

_____

_____

_____

Imagine a relative of yours—say, your aunt—is dying, and asks you to leave as her bequest a large sum of money to another relative, who already happened to be well off. You promise to do so, and your aunt dies. Nobody else knows about this money or her request. Would you be justified in donating the money to a homeless shelter instead?

_____

_____

_____

Imagine you promised to pay some kids down the street to take care of your pets and yard while you're out of town. Once you're back, you look at the money you're about to pay them and realize that it would make more of a difference to the homeless. Would you be justified in telling the kids that you're sorry . . . but they're not getting paid?

_____

_____

The Philosophy

Of course, Kant's theory about the basis of morality is not the only one around. It's the utilitarian theory of John Stuart Mill (1806–1873) that seems closest to common sense to most of us today. The "utility" in "utilitarianism" just refers to anything with usefulness for anyone—so if it helps with anyone's life, liberty, or pursuit of happiness, it counts. Utilitarianism, then, is the idea that we ought to act to maximize utility. So, the right action to take is the one that best serves the most of everyone's needs, desires, and goals—as Mill put it in his bumper-sticker version: the greatest good for the greatest number. (Okay, bumper stickers weren't actually around in nineteenth-century England, but that's not the point.)

Acting on the basis of the greatest good for the greatest number fits pretty well with our ideas of right and wrong, for the most part, but things can get strange. If we think about utilitarian calculation carelessly, it starts to look like we can justify any amount of lying and cheating if it helps the right number of people.

Consider the three questions we looked at previously. I'm guessing that you were much more comfortable with the first example, the one about the bequest to neo-Nazis, than with the third, about stiffing kids in favor of the homeless. What's the difference? Of course, there's a difference in the amount of good and the amount of harm, but there's also a difference in social trust. If we break our promises, then we undermine the trust and cooperation that our society depends upon. You might be helping the homeless, but you're not being a good neighbor, and you're not teaching those kids good values. We care about telling the truth because honesty is usually a great way of getting to the greatest good for the greatest number!

Exceptions, like the first example perhaps, are few and far between. Moral rules are important for the utilitarian, but because ultimately they're important *only* because they *tend* to maximize benefits for people, there can be some exceptions.

Harm for the Greater Good

Imagine you see a trolley rolling toward five people who have been tied to the track. You don't have any way of stopping the trolley, but you can switch it to a different track. There's only one person tied to that alternate track. Should you throw the switch? Why?

_____

_____

_____

Imagine there's no switch, but this time, you do have something nearby that could stop the trolley: a very fat man. If you push him onto the track, the trolley would derail after hitting him, and save the five people tied to the track. Should you?

_____

_____

_____

Forget the trolleys. Imagine instead that a terrorist group has claimed that they will set off a bomb that will kill at least five people. You have a member of the group in custody, but he refuses to talk. Should you resort to torture if doing so will get you information that will allow you to stop the attack? Why or why not?

_____

_____

_____

The Philosophy

These are troubling questions, and if you really think about what it would be like to make the call, it might be hard to imagine throwing the switch (or the fat man) even if you're convinced that it's the right thing to do.

The reason why ethicists have played around with these examples—the first originally comes from Philippa Foot (1920–2010), and the second from Judith Jarvis Thomson (1929–)—is that "thought experiments" like these help to isolate our moral intuitions and understand why we believe what we believe.

We're much more likely to find it acceptable to switch tracks than to throw the fat man on the rails, even though the losses and gains are the same in both cases. But why? Some claim it's because in the first case we're just reacting to a situation in progress, and all six people are already inside the situation, whereas in the second case we're adding someone uninvolved into the situation,

which makes us feel more responsible. But how important should our feeling of responsibility be compared to saving lives? Another theory is that in the second case we're actively intending someone's death, whereas in the first, the death of the single person on the other track is just a kind of side effect of saving the five.

The third example seems the same, but only if we accept the terms of the thought experiment. In reality, you might not be sure that there is actually a bomb at all. Or maybe you won't be able to stop the attack anyway. Or you could get bad information from the alleged terrorist—people being tortured will confess to things they didn't do. The real-life circumstances are much more uncertain and complicated than thought experiments, and taking harmful action is very difficult to justify, even in circumstances that seem most in its favor.

Animal Rights

Imagine you're in charge of making the final choice about where to put up a dam to create a reservoir for a municipal water supply. One valley is used occasionally by hikers. Another is almost never visited but is the nesting ground of a particular bird species, which would be displaced by the reservoir. How do you weigh the inconvenience to the hikers against that to the birds? Does the birds' happiness have moral weight?

_____

_____

_____

Cage-free eggs are just a dollar or two more expensive than factory-farmed eggs, and they're right next to one another in the grocery store. What benefit do you (or would you) get from those dollars? Is that benefit enough to outweigh the suffering of chickens who live out their lives in cramped, disease-ridden conditions? Why, or why not?

_____

_____

_____

Veal comes from young calves separated from their mothers and kept physically inactive to keep their meat tender. Can the experience of eating veal justify this treatment? Why or why not?

_____

_____

_____

The Philosophy

If we adopt the utilitarian view that the right action is the one that produces the greatest good for the greatest number, then we just need to do a kind of cost-benefit analysis to figure out how best to act. For each possible choice, we add up the happiness of each individual benefited and then subtract the suffering of each individual harmed. We can then take whichever action has the greatest net benefit (or, if all our options are bad, whichever action has the least net loss). But who counts as an individual? Do birds count, for example? Do we weigh their happiness as heavily as that of a person?

Australian philosopher Peter Singer (1946–) thinks we can account for this using his "preference utilitarianism." What counts for him are preferences that can either be met or denied. This allows him to set up a kind of moral spectrum among animals. People have all kinds of preferences—not just suffering and pleasure, but plans for the future, desires, intellectual enjoyment, furthering our causes and values in the world,

and so on. Other animals, like dogs and cats, can't have, for example, political causes or favorite pastimes, and this limits the range of preferences they can have. Still other creatures, like clams or insects, have very limited preferences, perhaps limited to preferring not to suffer.

For Singer, animals count insofar as they are able to have preferences, and this is sufficient to allow us to compare the limited but serious preferences of nonhuman animals, like those in the questions you answered, against the less limited (but often trivial) preferences of humans. As soon as we set up any such grounds for interspecies comparison, Singer thinks we should immediately realize that veal is obviously unacceptable, that cage-free eggs are certainly worth the extra dollar, and that animals need to be included in all sorts of public policy choices. As we'll talk about later, in Chapter 11: Death, it also has some implications for our responsibilities to different kinds of humans, like fetuses and the brain dead.

The Childhood Hero

Make a short list of people you admired when you were growing up. Try to think of people who inspired you at different ages.

1. _____
2. _____
3. _____
4. _____

What about these people made them important to you?

1. _____
2. _____
3. _____
4. _____

How do you think your attachment to each of them influenced your development?

1. _____
2. _____
3. _____
4. _____

The Philosophy

Modern ethical theory concentrates on how to act, but the ancient Greeks were more concerned with who you should *be*—character rather than choices. We still think about this issue today, of course, and philosophers continue to think about these questions of character, most often by returning to Aristotle's theory of virtues.

Having a virtuous character means that you have a habit and inclination to do virtuous things—being courageous, for example, means you're likely to take the right action even when it's dangerous to do so. How do you become virtuous? By making virtuous choices, and developing the habit of doing so. We become moderate in our eating, for example, by making healthy choices—eventually, the urge to stuff our faces recedes, and we become better people, less driven by our desires.

We can use reason to help develop good habits and virtuous character. The principle of "moderation in all things" helps us find courage between the extremes of cowardice and foolhardy impulse; healthy desires between the extremes of self-hating abstinence and being driven by gluttony or lust.

Very often, though, the path to virtue comes not by abstract reasoning, but through a moral exemplar—a role model that we admire, and seek to emulate. How much have the character traits you value in yourself been brought about by careful thought, and how much by emotional connections to people who represented those traits for you? Even when we become disillusioned about a role model, as we often do—perhaps this is part of what it is to become an adult—we owe much to the people we thought others were, and we seek to embody the virtues we thought we saw in them.

Care and the Limits of Justice

Imagine you're judging a talent show for elementary school students, and your child is competing. Is there any reasonable way you could justify choosing your child as the winner, if you believe another child had put on a better performance?

_____

_____

_____

Now imagine that a fire breaks out. There's not enough time to get every child to safety. Are you justified in rescuing your child rather than another child who is nearer to you and whom you are more likely able to save? After all, that child has parents who love her too. Is your child more important than theirs?

_____

_____

_____

What about buying your child a new toy, when the same money could be spent funding vaccinations that could save a child's life in Africa? Is this form of favoritism moral?

_____

_____

_____

The Philosophy

Modern ethical theories like Kantianism and Utilitarianism focus on justice and impartiality. While this focus leads us well in many ways and helps us explain why we believe what we believe about right and wrong, in some situations impartiality can seem immoral. Theories of morality that emphasize impartiality struggle to make sense of why we think it is not only acceptable, but moral and appropriate to show favoritism to those nearest and dearest to us.

A recent movement in ethical theory—the ethics of care—offers an alternate, corrective account of morality. Feminist theorists noted that the ethics of justice and impartiality were grounded in public life and policy choice—traditionally male domains—while ignoring the ethical realms of home and family—traditionally feminine aspects of the moral life. It is certainly a sign of how male dominated our society has been that ethical theorists did not view as a fatal flaw that the ethics of justice are contradicted by everyday life within domains associated more with women than men.

By setting up care as a fundamental moral category, we can begin to make sense of why we think partiality has a rightful place in a moral life. It's not that women have "care" and men have "justice"—men and women participate in both, of course. However, we have overemphasized justice and failed to appreciate care, just as we have overvalued the stereotypically male domains of work and government and undervalued the stereotypically female domains of friendship, hearth, and home. Working out the proper balance of justice and care, and in which situations one or the other ought to determine our actions, is not an easy matter, but it's a good starting point to recognize that impartiality by itself is clearly not enough to stand alone as the basis for a moral life.

Christianity: A Morality of Weakness?

The Christian Bible teaches to love one's enemies, that the meek shall inherit the earth, and that it is easier for a camel to fit through the eye of a needle than for a rich man to enter heaven. Does this mean that Christianity teaches us to be complacent, subservient, and poor? If not, why not?

_____

_____

_____

_____

Do these teachings help us become better people, or easier to control—or both? Why? Give an example.

_____

_____

_____

_____

How can a Christian justify being wealthy or powerful?

_____

_____

_____

_____

The Philosophy

Friedrich Nietzsche claimed that Christian morality is a reflection of the wretched and oppressed position of Jews and early Christians under Roman rule. He saw in it a "slave mentality" that was based in resentment. These oppressed peoples looked to their masters and saw that they held every benefit that was denied to the oppressed and enslaved. The masters had wealth, power, strength, health, vitality, conviction, and purpose. Unable to act on their hatred of the masters due to their weakness, they projected this resentment—too painful to hold on to while they were so impotent—onto the world itself through the idea of God's judgment. It is as if they said, "I don't hate you—I love you, my enemy. But God hates you, and will punish you for having everything good that I lack."

The result, according to Nietzsche, is that Christianity, defined by its resentment of these natural goods, becomes a religion that preaches weakness and hatred toward the values of the world—so much so that Christian ascetics took to whipping themselves, living as hermits, and denying themselves the pleasures of food and drink. This, in Nietzsche's view, is why Christianity preaches that we should deny the value of this world and view the pleasures of the body as evil; Christianity is based in the resentment of slaves toward their masters, and this slave mentality continued even after Christians came to dominate Europe.

Today, however, we might ask why so many American Christians seem to ignore these calls for humility, poverty, and service. One possible biblical justification for seeking wealth is "The Parable of the Talents," which some Christians interpret to be literally about money rather than a parable about God's gifts. But it seems strange to me to interpret this parable literally when most parables are interpreted metaphorically—especially considering that it is so much in conflict with so many other biblical teachings about wealth and worldly power.

Christianity and Standing
for the Downtrodden

We recognize the value of "turning the other cheek" as it is usually understood: refusing to meet violence with violence. But does turning the other cheek mean that we (or at least that Christians) should allow oppression to continue? How can we reconcile the idea with resistance?

_____

_____

_____

Choosing on your own to overlook offenses against you seems noble. But what about attacks against others? Is it noble to "turn the other cheek" when you see a wrong done to someone else? Why or why not?

_____

_____

_____

What about actions or words against you that affect others indirectly? If you were a minority, (or if, in fact, you are one), would you turn the other cheek when someone insults you for your race? Would doing so be noble, or would you be failing to do your part in standing up to abuse and hatred that also harms your sisters and brothers?

_____

_____

_____

The Philosophy

Walter Wink (1935–2012), a Christian theologian, gave a compelling but too-little-known account of Jesus's Sermon on the Mount that provides an understanding of these elements of Christian ethics in line with nonviolent resistance, and similar to the ideals and practices of Martin Luther King Jr., and the American Civil Rights movement.

If we understand the real-life meaning of the claims in the Sermon on the Mount in historical and cultural context, these questions can be resolved. Then as today, striking someone with the back of your hand expressed contempt and superiority. If you think about the physical act of turning your left cheek to someone who has struck you on the right, you can see that, if the Jews listening to Jesus did so when they were struck by a Roman, the Roman would be forced to either use his left hand—which was considered improper—or hit with a fist or open hand. Far from being submissive, turning the other cheek forces the Roman to attack the Jew as an equal instead of using the back-

hand, and makes a strong political claim of equality and worth without resorting to violence or retaliation.

Jesus also advised to "give the shirt off your back" in a time when being naked in public was shameful. Debt holders were legally allowed to demand cloaks from those unable to pay. By advising Jews to give their shirts as well, Wink claimed, Jesus showed how the Jews could demonstrate that they had been insulted and oppressed by purposefully debasing themselves. In the same way, people in occupied territories could be forced by Romans to carry their packs for a mile— but *only* a mile. By "walking an extra mile," as Jesus advised, Jews could take control of the situation, and through overcompliance, implicate the soldier in breaking the law!

In this understanding, Jesus didn't teach passivity at all, but *passive resistance*. What has been interpreted as a moral teaching of weakness was really a political teaching about insisting on equality and standing against injustice.

CHAPTER 4

✳

Political Justice

The question of who, if anyone, should rule is an ancient one, but I've limited our discussion here to concerns relevant to the representative democratic governments common today. The topics have an American emphasis as well, but the issues should be recognizable and entirely relevant to anyone living in a democratic republic.

The fundamental issue with democracy has been the same since Plato's time: The people are basically a bunch of idiots. If you think that's harsh, imagine you're in Walmart. Look around and consider whether you want those people making choices about your life. And here's the kicker: They'd say the same thing about you. And each other. And yet we all think that our *own* views should be represented!

This is the shortest chapter in the book, and is the first of two chapters on justice. If you're reading this with a book club or Socrates Café, it might make sense to look at the two together as one large chapter of thirteen entries instead of two smaller ones (of five and eight entries, respectively).

The True Ship Captain

Running for political office is a disruptive, difficult, expensive process. How much do you think politicians are motivated by idealism, and how much by a desire for control?

_____

_____

_____

_____

There are a great many people—economists, policy analysts, scholars of poverty, etc.—who are experts on issues of great concern for the nation. Why aren't they in office?

_____

_____

_____

_____

What kind of people do you want in office and how could we get them there? Why would they be more effective than those who are currently in office?

_____

_____

_____

_____

The Philosophy

To live together, we need to make choices that balance the needs and desires of some against those of others. Even some anarchists recognize this need—their view is that these systems of power and control should be momentary, limited, and local; not that we can make it without ever having someone making tough calls. Given this broad agreement that we need "deciders in chief," who should they be?

Plato used the famous analogy of the "ship of state" to address this. He asked us to imagine a ship at sea—someone has to take the helm! Among those who clamor to take control, each has his motivation to try to be captain. Some seek to steer the ship because they believe they know what's best; others seek control out of pride or because they are power hungry. Look away from the fray now, and imagine a useless stargazer. He does not seek control or power, but is interested only in looking to the skies and seeing the constancy and change among the stars. Here, Plato says, is the true ship captain. Only he knows the stars, which are the right basis for steering the ship—only he knows how to use the pole star to find north, to guide the ship along its route and then back to port.

For the same reasons, he claimed, the philosophers should rule the state. It is they who care about truth and seek out the reality of things, which should be the proper basis for making decisions. Those who seek power do not deserve it, and those who deserve it do not seek it. But should we, as Plato thought, make philosophers kings, and make all others subject to their rule? For those of us who believe in the value of democracy, Plato's problem is real and serious, but his solution is hard to accept.

To Refine and Enlarge

In the simplest form of "direct democracy" we would simply vote on everything. In this system, would the many poor simply vote to take and distribute the wealth of the rich? Would the majority simply vote to remove rights from racial or other minorities? Do you think direct democracy would lead to greater justice or greater injustice? Why?

_____

_____

_____

_____

_____

_____

In a representative democracy, we sometimes speak of elected officials as "employees" of those they represent, whose job is simply to bring their public's opinions into legislation. Does this bring up the same "mob rule" problems as direct democracy might?

_____

_____

_____

_____

_____

The Philosophy

The idea of self-rule is pretty uncontroversial today, but there's a basic problem with the very idea of democracy: Under majority rule, the minority is subject to the will of the majority—and if the majority doesn't care about the minority, the minority can't use majority rule to protect itself!

In *The Federalist Papers*, written during public debate about whether to ratify the Constitution of the United States, Alexander Hamilton (1755–1804), James Madison (1751–1836), and John Jay (1745–1829) took up this problem of "faction." While the starting assumption is clearly that self-rule through democracy is best and most just, Federalist 10 recognized that "no man is allowed to be a judge in his own cause," and that there is a constant threat of faction—a voting bloc acting on mere self-interest—in a democratic system. The solution, according to James Madison in Federalist 10, is representative democracy in a democratic republic. By having choices made by a congress of representatives, the public will can be "refined and enlarged" by being placed into the collective consideration of this small group of public-minded patriots, concerned for the good of the nation. A similar balance is struck between the Senate and House, as described in Federalist 63: The House is subject to frequent elections so that its members are forced to remain true to the direct and stated will of the people. Senators, on the other hand, are elected for a longer term so they are able to make choices that might be unpopular but pay off in the end, and bring about changes that take a series of connected laws and measures that require planning for more than a year or two at a stretch.

In today's media environment, however, we have detailed day-by-day coverage of what happens in Congress, and elections have spread out so that representatives are almost constantly in "campaign mode." This is clearly good for transparency and responsiveness but bad for making good but unpopular choices. Thus we have begun to see the return of the problems of "mob rule" and faction that our representative republican structure was meant to solve.

Consumer Democracy

Imagine you're against all wars, or opposed to any corporate influence in government. Who can you vote for? What can you do to get your view represented?

_____

_____

_____

Imagine, like many Catholics, that you are in favor of social programs that help the poor, but against war, and against abortion rights. Which party can you call your own? How can you decide which lives to support through your vote, and which to abandon?

_____

_____

_____

In preferential or instant-runoff voting, you rank your choices for office. If your first choice doesn't win, your vote goes to your second choice, so that voting for a "minor party" candidate isn't "throwing your vote away." How much of a difference would this make for you? Why do you suppose we don't use preferential voting?

_____

_____

_____

_____

The Philosophy

The Federalist entrusted representatives to place local and factional needs and desires into a wider context, and to moderate current passions by long-term goals. Another possibility is that we, the people, could refine and enlarge our views in this way on our own. Are we so mired within our self-interest that we are incapable of having reasonable, careful discussion with one another and come to agreements on our own, rather than delegating these hard choices to representatives? Surely, this seems hopeless in our current political environment, but it hasn't always been this way, and it need not remain so.

The German philosopher Jürgen Habermas (1929–) has done historical work showing how a "public sphere" emerged in the eighteenth century through dialogue and debate in coffeehouses and newspapers throughout Europe. People had the time, information, and communicative opportunities to engage in thoughtful public debate about the politics of the day, and it became possible for there to be such a thing as "public opinion," rather than merely individual or official state perspectives.

Things have gone downhill since then. Today we have fallen away from a deliberative democracy, in which we engage in public debate and decision making, to a merely consumer democracy, where we as citizens simply choose between the options presented. In this situation, the media is focused on the horse race and party-line pugilism rather than on thoughtful public discussion. Even preferential voting wouldn't change this, but breaking the two-part duopoly would at least open up the debate to more options and ideas. The road to a political culture in which we all engage in discussion about issues and policy rather than candidates and party platforms will be a long one.

The Phone Book Solution

Recent estimates are that about 4 percent of households in the United States have a net worth of a million dollars or more, but that nearly half of the members of Congress are millionaires. What effect, if any, do you think this has on our elected representatives' ability to represent us?

_____

_____

_____

_____

Founders of the United States intended political representation to be a kind of public service that citizens would make for a time, then returning to their regular lives. Americans today are suspicious of "career politicians." Would things be improved if we limited all elected officials to a single term of office? Why or why not?

_____

_____

_____

_____

The Philosophy

What makes philosophy distinctive is its willingness to consider any possibility, and to call into question even things that seem natural and commonsense, to see whether they are merely something we're used to or if they can stand on their own merits. Sometimes, in desperation, we think we'd get better politicians by picking names at random from the phone book. Well—why not? Seriously.

This is the model we use for jury duty. We have the idea that justice is often best served by including a jury of people chosen at random, rather than leaving guilt or innocence to experts or "career jurists." In ancient Athens, not just juries but *most* governmental offices were filled by lottery, and some contemporary writers, like Ernest Callenbach (1929–2012), have discussed the possibility of returning to this seemingly radical idea.

How radical is the idea, really? If we believe in democratic ideals, shouldn't we want choices to be made by regular people? Of course, on the face of it, we might imagine people just legislating based on their own limited knowledge and prejudices, but the checks and balances could help to ensure that the close-mindedness of a few can't take over, and more responsible citizen-legislators could draw on the knowledge and research of experts, just like juries choose based on expert evidence and argumentation.

Elections support party politics rather than open debate and deliberation. The expense of elections means that poor people are unlikely to gain office. The need for campaign donations gives undue influence to the interests of corporations and wealthy individuals. Would we be better off without having elections at all? Are elections, on the whole, good or bad for democracy?

Rule by Nobody

The U.S. subprime mortgage crisis played a significant role in the global finan-cial crisis from which we are still trying to recover. Mortgages were written for people unable to meet payments, sold to investment banks, and trenched and repackaged as mortgage-based securities, purchased by investors. Many investment bankers made huge amounts of money from the bubble, and when it crashed it nearly brought down the U.S. economy. For each of the following involved parties, what's the strongest case that can be made that they're the ones to blame for what happened, and what's their strongest defense against taking the blame?

- *Homebuyers: _____*

- *Loan officers: _____*

- *Mortgage company CEOs: _____*

- *Investment banks: _____*

- *Financial regulators: _____*

- *Investment rating agencies: _____*

- *Investors: _____*

The Philosophy

We typically view a form of government as more tyrannical if it has fewer people responsible for making important decisions—aristocracy is more tyrannical than democracy, and monarchy is more tyrannical than aristocracy. If this is true, wrote German-Jewish philosopher Hannah Arendt (1906–1975), then our society today is the most tyrannical possible, because contemporary bureaucratic governance can be rightly called Rule by Nobody. In this case, we can easily imagine everyone's excuses. And, as much as everyone in that list is responsible for what happened in the sense that it wouldn't have happened without them, it seems clear that it's not exactly any one party's *fault*.

What Arendt saw in Nazi Germany—the soldier "just following orders," the German citizen trusting the government, the bookkeepers running numbers and not asking what they represent—she saw throughout bureaucratic society. At the bottom, we don't have the perspective to understand what we're doing; we "just work here." At the top, we have to make choices for the sake of the investors. As investors, we usually don't even know what companies we've invested in—we just want a return. It's nobody's responsibility to ask whether what's happening is right—and, worse, no one even seems to have the ability to take effective action against the system, even if she wants to take responsibility.

And government? So long as we think government is there just to support business and foster economic growth, government is just another part of this system. Government's role is limited to producing a good climate for growth, and any effort to take responsibility by promoting the interest of people or the environment tends to be viewed as "excessive regulation" and "the nanny state"—right up until the point when we have nationwide foreclosures, health epidemics, financial collapse, or irremediable environmental damage.

CHAPTER 5

✳

Economic Justice

Economic justice includes a great many things, but here we'll focus on equal opportunity in employment, ownership, the right to profits, the right to interest, and wealth distribution. This is one place where we see the views of many philosophers at variance with public opinion. There was a time when we had arguments and debates about the fundamental issues behind markets and property rights, but we rarely do today. Instead, we tend to just assume that the property rights we're used to must be good and must be justifiable somehow or other, because they've been around for a while. This is not to say that our current structures of late capitalism are unjustifiable, but rather that we just haven't spent much time justifying them. Decisions are often made by established interests in order to further their interests, and lawmakers have been at least as likely to help out big business and the wealthy (i.e., campaign donors) as they are to follow an issue of principle.

To give one example that my students seem to find more and more outrageous with each passing year, consider the "justice" of recent changes in intellectual property rights. Why did we need to extend copyright past the author's death? Is that going to encourage writers and musicians to work more? Why did lawmakers give corporate-owned intellectual property *more* protection than works owned by actual people? In this example, as with many others, when we look for justifications for our current systems, we find them flimsy, missing, or decrepit. And when we ask about what would be just, we sometimes find ourselves going off in some unfamiliar directions.

Privilege

Talk to a friend who is of a different race. Ask her what her race has meant to her, and how she believes it has influenced how she has been perceived and treated. Share your own experiences as well.

_____

_____

_____

_____

What about your friend's experience is most surprising to you? Have you ever experienced something similar?

_____

_____

_____

_____

How has your experience of the social meaning of your race been different? What has been easier for you, and what has been more difficult?

_____

_____

_____

_____

The Philosophy

In a 2004 study, University of Chicago professor Marianne Bertrand and Harvard professor Sendhil Mullainathan found that identical résumés sent to job ads in Boston and Chicago got 50 percent more calls for interviews if the names at the top were Emily and Greg than if they were Lakisha and Jamal. This is but one bit of evidence among a multitude of empirical demonstrations that our society continues to be racist and sexist, even though, today, almost nobody thinks that racism and sexism are acceptable.

One of the most significant reasons why people who aren't racist do racist things is confirmation bias. We internalize cultural images and associations: Latinos on TV are often drug dealers in crime dramas; the woman of the house is already there when the sitcom kids get home from school; Asian people play stringed instruments. These internalized images condition how we interpret others, even if we don't believe that they represent anything real or meaningful. The mind, like everything else, tends to follow the path of least resistance, and stereotypes pave the way for confirmation bias. You can feel this at work for yourself by taking an Implicit Assumptions Test—Harvard's Project Implicit has some very good ones online (*www.implicit.harvard.edu*).

This is one important aspect of white privilege and male privilege. Women and minorities are attached to all sorts of associations, often negative ones, whereas whites and men have the privilege of being much more likely to be judged on their own merits. There's much more to privilege than this, though. Behavior that might be called efficient and "no-nonsense" among white men might get a woman labeled "bitch," or a minority "angry." Being a white male means that wherever you go, the people in charge are likely to be like you, and if you do something wrong it's taken to be your own mistake rather than the inevitable consequence of your race or gender. Even claiming that there is no privilege is a form of privilege—it's easy not to notice privilege when it's in your favor, but trying to be "race blind" is a poor solution when others are making *your* race an issue.

Preferential Hiring

Does the best-qualified person always deserve to get the job? Why? What exceptions to this general principle can you think of, if any?

_____

_____

_____

_____

_____

_____

Using your insights on experiences of race, from the last question, consider what it would be like to be a white applicant passed over in order to hire a less-qualified minority, and what it would be like to be a minority applicant passed over in order to hire a less-qualified white. How would these similar acts take on different meanings, based on what it's like to be a minority in our society and what it's like to be white?

_____

_____

_____

_____

_____

_____

The Philosophy

Affirmative action is very controversial among Americans, but not nearly as much so among philosophers. Author and Professor Emeritus at the University of California, Santa Cruz, Richard Wasserstrom's defense of programs of preferential treatment has been influential and illustrates clearly the kinds of considerations that make this seem like an easy issue to many of us.

First, there's the charge of "reverse racism." The problem with this, according to Wasserstrom, is that what's wrong with racism is not that it uses an irrelevant characteristic to judge others, but that it's a systematic program to *create and maintain* inequality. Programs of preferential treatment also use an irrelevant characteristic to make decisions, but they are systematic programs to *reduce* inequality—and this seems like an important difference! Even if there's always something troubling about considering race, this alone shows us that calling preferential treatment "reverse racism" only makes sense if you consider individual justice but ignore social justice, and the wrong of racism is surely an issue of social justice.

Even if it's necessary for social justice, there's still clearly something unfair to the rejected individual in preferential hiring. But what kind of fairness are you entitled to? Fundamentally, businesses own their money and can do what they want with it. Your qualifications do not entitle you to a job—so long as they aren't perpetuating social injustices, businesses are free to make choices that they think will be most profitable, and that often means preferential hiring. Having a diverse workforce is a benefit in a diverse society, and the distinctive experiences of women and minorities can be a benefit as well. Further, a less-qualified candidate may be the better candidate—it may be more impressive to have achieved slightly less in the face of greater difficulties than to have achieved slightly more while enjoying white and male privilege.

The Invisible Hand

We typically recognize that we can achieve more by cooperating with others, and working together. What sense does it make that production in our society is based instead on competition?

_____

_____

_____

The way we live today makes us dependent on others for food, water, housing, and energy. Why do we allow those providing goods necessary for life to "skim off the top"? Why not provide these goods on a nonprofit basis?

_____

_____

_____

We say "it takes money to make money," and surely having a greater initial investment makes success and market dominance more likely. Doesn't that mean that the rich, on the whole, get richer, and the poor generally stay poor? If so, is that a good way to run a society?

_____

_____

_____

_____

The Philosophy

Maybe you said that the way we're doing things is wrong, but if you tried to justify our capitalist mode of production, it's likely that what you said was some version of the idea of the Invisible Hand.

This concept is that through free competition in a transparent and open market, based on profit motive, we see a maximally efficient use of resources and an improved standard of living that benefits everyone. A business that charges too much will be undercut by a competitor. If a production process is inefficient, a competitor will figure out a better way so it can sell the product for less and take over the market. By acting in our self-interest in this competitive environment, it is argued, we end up with better results for everyone than we would have if we planned things out and tried to help people.

The Scottish moral and economic philosopher Adam Smith (1723–1790) first formulated the idea, but important parts of his view get lost today. For one thing, this action of the market was meant to be a protection against selfishness, whereas today it is given as a *justification* of selfishness! Also, today we tend to talk about profits as something capitalists have a *right* to take, but for Smith, profits were justified only as a useful means to create a prosperous and just society.

Smith's vision of what that society would look like is also different from what we'd expect. In his *Theory of Moral Sentiments*, he argued that the rich would be "led by an invisible hand to make nearly the same distribution of the necessaries of life, which would have been made, had the earth been divided into equal portions among all its inhabitants."

If Adam Smith saw the inequality of our society, our rampant selfishness, and the massive profits of corporations, he would regard capitalism as a failed moral experiment—in this regard, at least.

Property Rights

If profit-driven competition doesn't always result in the greatest good for society, is there another justification for a company taking profits? Don't we have a right to profit from our efforts? If so, why? Even if it seems obvious, try to explain it.

_____

_____

_____

What are the limits of our property rights? Is it acceptable, as in eminent domain laws, to force people to sell their homes at fair prices if the land is needed for social utility, like building a new airport? What about for economic prosperity, like building a new factory or sports stadium?

_____

_____

_____

If we have a right to our property, then taxes require moral justification. If you thought it was okay to force the sale of property for an airport, does that also justify taxes for social utilities? What about taxes that are meant to support businesses—like shifting the tax burden away from corporations and investors through incentives and lowered tax rates, and relying more on revenue sources like income and sales taxes?

_____

_____

_____

The Philosophy

The moral justification of capitalism is sometimes also traced back to English philosopher John Locke (1632–1704). Unlike Adam Smith, who argued for free-market competition based on the greater good for all of society, Locke argued that we have a God-given individual right to our property. On this kind of basis, whether it's best for society is irrelevant—it's our right, and that's the bottom line.

Locke argued that although the world was given to humanity in common, we were given our own bodies individually. This is why we can control our bodies with our minds, and, try as we might, we can't control anything else that way. Based on this, he argued that whatever we mix our bodies with—as we do by expending the hours we have to walk the earth improving something through our labor—becomes rightly our sole property, so long as we leave enough of nature for others to do the same. So if you make some clothes from fabric, or even just pick some berries out in the forest, you've mixed your labor with it and it becomes your right to keep or sell it, and to profit from your work.

There's been some question of what a Lockean view implies about eminent domain. At the time that Locke was writing, if you didn't own anything, you could just go to the uncharted wilds of America and till the soil. Today, it's not clear that there's "enough and as good" of raw nature for us to go out and improve through our labor. The fact that almost the entire planet is already owned by someone makes an absolute right to property more questionable, and the idea of eminent domain seems more necessary.

There are debates about what Lockean theory means for taxation as well. If we're going to have public goods and works (e.g., roads), it seems only fair that everyone should help pay for them. But if our right to property is God given, then how can it be just to force anyone to give up any of his property?

On Interest and Investment

If we agree with Locke that property rights are based on labor, how are we justified in charging interest on a loan? Does labor justify taking profits on someone's borrowing from us—if not, does anything justify charging interest?

_____

_____

_____

On the assumption that there is some justification for charging interest, are we justified in charging more to the poor and desperate? If our property rights are absolute, can we justify laws against predatory lending—payday loans at very high rates, for example?

_____

_____

_____

Based on your answers to the previous questions, consider making an investment. Are you entitled to profits from someone else's work because you supplied startup funding? Given that these profits come from someone else's labor, isn't she entitled to keep them? If not, how much of the profits are you entitled to, and why?

_____

_____

_____

The Philosophy

These are some serious problems with justifying capitalist profit taking based on Locke's labor-desert theory. We might say that the labor bound up in having accumulated wealth in the first place justifies taking further profits by charging interest—but then we're left explaining why the person doing the work doesn't at least equally deserve those profits. A further problem is that many of the members of our "investment class" have inherited their wealth; it seems difficult to say that the labor of one's ancestors justifies taking a profit on lending out that wealth. Those born wealthy start to seem like mere parasites who contribute nothing while reaping profits from others. A better answer might be to appeal to the greater good, and say that we need these economic tools to keep our system going—but then we have to ask whether the greater good is served by structures that tend to help the rich get richer while keeping the poor poor.

While there has been a recent upsurge in resentment against bankers and financiers, we are still more accepting of these financial arrangements than we have been in the past, when charging interest was known as the sin of *usury*. St. Thomas Aquinas wrote that "to take usury for money lent is unjust in itself, because this is to sell what does not exist, and this evidently leads to inequality which is contrary to justice." The money has its own value, printed on its face. To charge more than that amount for it is to charge both for the object and its use, as if we sold someone a bottle of wine, but demanded an additional payment if the buyer decided to drink it.

John Calvin (1509–1564), the Protestant reformer, thought that there were fair ways of charging interest, but that for the most part "the practice of usury and the killing of men" are justly placed "in the same rank of criminality, for the object of this class of people is to suck the blood of other men," and "men should not cruelly oppress the poor, who ought rather to receive sympathy and compassion."

Corporate Social Responsibility

Ford Motor Company produced the Pinto, which had a design flaw that made the car prone to catch on fire, especially when in rear-end collisions. Ford determined that the cost of a recall, plus the $11 per car it would take to repair the issue, was greater than the likely cost of lawsuits brought by those injured and the families of those killed in these preventable accidents, and determined not to do the recall. Did they make the right call? Why or why not?

_____

_____

_____

_____

If it's profitable to do so, should a public company pollute as much and as often as is legally allowed? Why or why not?

_____

_____

_____

Given that public companies have an obligation to give investors a return on their investments, what kinds of public interests are sufficient reasons to sacrifice profits for?

_____

_____

_____

The Philosophy

Nobel Prize–winning economist Milton Friedman (1912–2006) argued that public companies are the legal property of shareholders and therefore should be run based on shareholders' interests alone—and Friedman says it's fair to assume that the shareholders' only interest is profits. On this "shareholder theory" of corporate social responsibility, the corporation has an obligation to (legally) maximize profits no matter what. Any compromise of profitability for whatever purpose—helping the environment, paying employees well, donating to social causes—he compared to a form of taxation without representation; the CEO is basically taking someone else's money and spending it on whatever he thinks is important, which is almost a kind of theft.

Friedman's view has been hugely influential and has taken hold among a great many people in business and among a great many legislators as well. This is despite the fact that a large part of the public finds it immoral, and the arguments in its favor have been widely and seriously questioned.

Different kinds of property come with different kinds of rights. The bank may "own" your house as a financial interest—the bank can repackage your mortgage as a collateralized debt obligation—but bank officials can't drop by to use your bathroom or improve your landscaping. Just because investors own the business in some sense doesn't mean they own it in every sense. In fact, under the LLC structure, Ford investors were not liable for Ford's actions even though they "owned" the company. Why should the company be solely responsible to investors when they are not held responsible for what it does on their behalf?

A larger point is that we can have a society without business, but there can be no business without a society. If business is dependent on its natural and social environment, then it makes sense that business would have an obligation to help maintain a prosperous society, a healthy educated workforce, and a business environment where the public generally trusts corporations.

The Veil of Ignorance

Gina Rinehart (1954–), who has been named the world's wealthiest woman, is estimated to earn $1 million every half-hour from her investments and from the mining company she took over after her father's death. She has also recently stated that she's worried about how Australia can remain competitive when Africans are willing to work for less than $2 per day and has suggested that Australia cut its minimum wage. Should we allow the free market to determine how wealthy the wealthiest in a society can be, and how poor the poorest should be?

_____

_____

_____

If we institute a minimum wage, governmental job training programs, or higher tax rates for top wage earners, we are limiting inequality and, in effect, redistributing wealth. How can we justify what arguably amounts to taking from the rich to help the poor?

_____

_____

_____

If we accept that this is justifiable, why not raise the minimum wage to $30 per hour and raise the marginal tax rate for income above $1 million to 95 percent? Is that going too far? Where is the line?

_____

_____

The Philosophy

American philosopher John Rawls (1921–2002) gave answers to these questions in 1971, using an argument that was so obviously powerful that it changed the debate about distributive justice. Rawls's argument is impossible to ignore today, whether you think it's right or wrong.

When we talk about economic distribution, there's a basic problem: consent. It seems unjust to take property in the name of justice without consent—even more so when we are taxing people at different rates. Now, what would you consent to if you didn't know who you were? Imagine you were under a "veil of ignorance" and didn't know your social class, race, gender, sexual orientation, or anything else. What kind of distribution of wealth and opportunity would you want in society, based purely on your own self-interest?

You don't want a slave society, even if the nonslaves are really well off, because you might be a slave. You're betting with your life, and you want to maximize your minimum outcome here, and play it safe. Okay, so what about total equality of wealth? That's a safer bet, but in a society without *some* inequality, people don't see hard work and innovation pay off, and that means that there's likely to be less prosperity overall. So you want some inequality, but how much? Remember, you're betting with your life here, so you'll want more and more inequality, but only so long as it continues to help the least among us. As soon as more inequality would come at the expense of the poor, it's not maximizing our minimum outcome anymore, so it's no longer your best, safest bet.

There's more to the argument than this, of course, but this is enough to give us an answer to our questions: We are justified in redistributing wealth to have the kind of inequality that benefits everybody—much less than we have today!—because it's what *any* rational person *would* want if she didn't know who she was. So if the rich don't consent, we can tell that that's *only* because they know that they got a lucky draw in our very unequal society.

Giving and Keeping

What have you spent money on during the past week that was more important than what that same amount of money would have meant to a hungry family, a homeless veteran, or a child in need of vaccines? Justify your choices.

_____

_____

_____

_____

Assume that you have an absolute right to your property and that you owe no consideration either to society or to any individuals. Just because you have the right not to help others by donating to humanitarian causes, does that make it moral for you to choose not to? Why?

_____

_____

_____

_____

If you give 10 percent of your income, why don't you give 15 percent; if 15 percent, why not 20 percent? Is the 101st suffering child less important than the first one—or the 1,001st?

_____

_____

The Philosophy

Of course, the clearest form of consent is actual, literal consent, not the merely conceptual-rational consent we get with Rawls. But the practical value of donation and other forms of voluntary giving has clear limitations. There are many who just don't care, or don't think they have any responsibility to do anything for people they don't know and aren't connected with, but even those of us who do donate and volunteer don't go as far as it seems we ought to.

Peter Singer, a contemporary Australian ethicist, has pursued this issue very effectively in journal articles, book chapters, and an excellent article published in the *New York Times Magazine* called "The Singer Solution to World Poverty." Remember the trolley examples from the chapter on Morals? Singer asks you to imagine that you've parked your car on some tracks and gone for a walk. You see a train coming and a child tied to the tracks. If you do nothing, the child dies, but there's a switch you can throw to divert the train so that it will destroy your car instead. What kind of monster wouldn't throw the switch? And yet, if we imagine the child is in Bangladesh instead of the train tracks, and the threat to her life is disease or famine instead of a train, then we seem to have no problem keeping the car and letting her die. In fact, we have no problem buying an overpriced corporate latte when five days of lattes would be enough, through Heifer International, to provide a family in Tanzania with a flock of chickens to raise, breed, and collect and sell eggs from, alleviating hunger, dependence, and poverty.

It's an ingenious thought experiment. You're not responsible for the child on the tracks. You don't owe her anything, and she has no right to your help. Can you justify standing by as the child dies? Can you justify spending money that could have been spent to save a life? According to Singer, although making the change may be tough, the right answer is simple: "Whatever money you're spending on luxuries, not necessities, should be given away."

CHAPTER 6

Human Nature

When we think about the dignity and value of humanity—our reason, logic, morality, humane care, understanding, expansive vision, and spirituality—it seems an insult and affront that our bodies should be made out of meat. It's really pretty disgusting, and very inappropriate. Reasoning moral beings . . . made sweaty and squishy soft—and with a strange impulse to rub against one another (but only in private, out of shame). "Man," as Arthur Schopenhauer (1788–1860) put it, "is a burlesque of what he should be."

And yet, of course, the mind *is* the meat, at least in some sense. We are our bodies, and yet we are not *only* our biology. We are animals, but unusual ones who have (arguably, at least) transcended our animality. What roles do our bodies play in our self-determination? What roles *should* they play?

A Dog's Life

Our biological drives are very simple, limited perhaps to seeking sustenance, comfort, play (games, music, dancing, etc.), friendship, and sex. How did things get so complicated?

_____

_____

_____

_____

What would a society directed purely to satisfying these basic interests look like?

_____

_____

_____

_____

Would you like to live there? Wouldn't it be possible for you to "drop out" of society, join a commune, and live a simpler, more natural life? Why (unless you do live on a commune) haven't you done so?

_____

_____

_____

The Philosophy

Diogenes the Cynic (412–323 B.C.E.)—in the Greek, that means "Diogenes the Dog"—thought that even back in ancient Greece, human society had made things far more complicated than they needed to be, and humans, he thought, pretended they were some greater and more special thing than they really were. He was known as "the dog" because he lived according to this belief. He slept in a large broken clay pot among the dogs in the street, for he saw that animals had no need of beds or to sleep in the dark. He kept few possessions: a cloak to wear, which he slept in, and a bag for food. He once walked through the marketplace while masturbating. When confronted about his crude behavior, he said that he wished he could dispel hunger in the same way, by rubbing his belly. At a banquet, he was ridiculed by others, who threw bones to him, as they would a begging animal. So he peed on them, embracing his animality as a virtue, where they intended it as an insult.

Although he used unusual and shocking methods of propounding his views about human vanity and the actual simplicity of human needs, he was recognized as a wise man, and at least one story about him is still widely known to us today: He once carried a lantern through the marketplace at midday, explaining "I am looking for a man." This is often retold as "looking for an honest man," but the meaning is the same: He was illustrating the futility of finding anyone honest about what it is to be human.

Another story that illustrates his strange brilliance is that Alexander the Great (356–323 B.C.E.), as his army moved through Greece, sought out Diogenes. Alexander found him sleeping on the side of a road and said that he had heard of Diogenes's wisdom and would give him anything he desired. As Alexander stood over him, Diogenes replied, "Stand out of my sun." Alexander left him there and is said to have commented, "If I were not Alexander the Great, I should wish to be Diogenes the Dog."

The Law of the Jungle

In some previous questions, we've assumed that God exists and that He has particular ideas about how we should be treating each other. Assume now that there is no god. Why should you care about others?

_____

_____

_____

_____

What kind of morality would evolutionary "survival of the fittest" create in herd animals like us?

_____

_____

_____

_____

Why do we believe in right and wrong? Is it in our nature, or in our culture?

_____

_____

_____

_____

The Philosophy

As Australian philosopher J. L. Mackie (1917–1981) pointed out in a famous article, "The Law of the Jungle," evolutionary "survival of the fittest" doesn't happen on an individual level but on a genetic level—so, although there is individual competition for mates and food and so forth, a great many species, including our own, compete in their larger environment by banding together. Selfishness might further an individual's interests, but genes that motivate us to look out for one another—an uncle to protect his niece or cousins, for example—are carried forth generation after generation because they create mutual benefits. The willingness to sacrifice your own interests or even your own life may not help *you* survive, but it helps that *gene* survive, and that's what matters evolutionarily, as Richard Dawkins showed in *The Selfish Gene*.

Consider an example of Dawkins's that Mackie used: a bird species parasitized by dangerous ticks. If each bird only looked after itself, they'd all die, because they can't remove the ticks from the backs of their own heads. So they groom one another. But they don't do so indiscriminately—if they did, we'd see a genetic variation of birds who allowed themselves to be groomed but who didn't waste time grooming other birds. Those birds would have more offspring and take over the society, which would then die out because not enough birds would be grooming one another to keep the tick population in check. The strategy that's evolutionarily stable is what's called "reciprocal altruism": to groom another bird unless you find out that it won't groom you back, and then to never groom that bird again.

This is the kind of evolutionarily established morality we would expect to (and do in fact) find in pack animals, including humans: "Be done by as you did." Of course, we are not merely our biology, and culture and logic may bring us to change our behavior, but there's good reason to believe that this strategy of reciprocal altruism forms the biological basis of human morality.

Authority in the Pack Mentality

When have you done something you believed was wrong because you were "just doing your job"? What would it have cost you to have done the right thing instead?

_____

_____

_____

_____

When have you stood up against procedure, authority, or orders from a superior in order to do what you believed was right? What was the deciding moment for you?

_____

_____

_____

_____

What strategies can you think of that would help you do the right thing in the future, and resist excusing yourself from doing something wrong by saying "Well, I just work here . . ."?

_____

_____

_____

_____

The Philosophy

In 1961, Stanley Milgram (1933–1984) conducted an experiment at Yale University to see how far people would go to obey authority against their own beliefs. Participants were told they would take part in a study on memory, in which they would read a list of words to the subject, ask the subject to remember the proper word pairs, and administer a shock whenever the subject got it wrong. The shocks increased in intensity as more answers were incorrect, and the strongest shocks were indicated to be dangerous or possibly fatal. The "subject" was an actor, although the participants did not know that. He screamed when the participants thought they were shocking him, and as the "shocks" became more intense, he complained of a heart condition and cried out to be let go and for the experiment to end. The participants were uncomfortable continuing, but were told that the experiment required them to go on. In Milgram's initial experiment and in later recreations of the experiment, almost two-thirds of participants continued to the maximum shock.

Milgram designed the experiment to understand better how the Holocaust could have happened. Is it really possible that so many horrors could have been perpetrated by people who, for the most part, were ordinary, seemingly decent people? The answer seems to be yes. The tendency to obey authority is so strong that many people can be induced with relatively little incentive to do things they believe are wrong.

David Luban, Alan Strudler, and David Wasserman, researchers at the Institute for Philosophy and Public Policy, extended this to the realm of business to see how decent people take part in corporate activities that injure, defraud, and kill. They suggest that we think about getting involved with bureaucracies the same way we think about drinking: Go in with the awareness that your judgment may be impaired once you're in the middle of things, and try to remain aware that you're not fully in control of your own behavior.

The Other

Picture someone in a position of power and authority—a president, prime minister, CEO, or doctor. In what ways do you think her gender affects how she is viewed and the level of respect given to her by those she directs?

_____

_____

_____

You probably didn't picture her as a woman until the second sentence of the previous question, even though the terms used in the first sentence were gender neutral and applied equally well to women. What differences in the lives of women does it make that we assume that those in positions of power and authority are men?

_____

_____

_____

We tend to talk about men as generic people: "he," "man," "mankind." For the next few days, whenever you talk about a generic person or anyone whose gender isn't known, try saying "she" instead of "he" or "they." Then write down here what you learned from the experiment.

_____

_____

_____

The Philosophy

In what is usually called the "first wave" of feminism, women focused on gaining rights previously given to men alone: for example, rights to vote, inherit property, and hold public office. In the second wave, starting in earnest in the 1960s, women struggled against inequalities that had more to do with social exclusions rather than actual laws limiting the rights of women. The legal right to have a career and live a public life either instead of or in addition to traditional roles means little so long as women are disrespected and so long as the public continues to believe that a woman's place is in the home.

The French philosopher Simone de Beauvoir's (1908–1986) 1949 book *The Second Sex*, a thorough investigation of the meaning of women's biology and history, played an influential role in the development of feminism. From the title itself we immediately get a sense of the basic view she advanced: Woman has been defined as secondary; man is generic, and woman is "Other." The Other is defined by opposition to the norm and as a kind of exception to it. In biology and medicine, as well as in views of history, and perhaps most of all in psychoanalytic theory, women are viewed as altered, incomplete, or mutilated men. At most, women are viewed as "separate but equal," allowing the illusion of parity while men are still viewed as the "real" members of "mankind," as the word itself indicates.

The story of how male and female roles emerged, and how women became the second of the two sexes, is long and complicated, and the solution of granting equal legal recognition is a paltry and insufficient fix when merely superimposed on this cultural history. We must also think through the Otherness of woman. Imagining woman rather than man as generic, as I asked you to do in the third question, is one way to discover how deeply seated the view of women as Other is, for women as much as for men.

Feminine Virtues

Leaving aside the question of rights—I hope it's safe to assume we all agree on equal rights—do you think women have more domestic urges than men, and that it's natural for women to more often be in caretaker roles than breadwinner roles?

_____

_____

_____

Is it "only natural" that we see more women in service jobs, early childhood education, and nursing, rather than in positions of more power and authority? Is this a problem we as a society ought to fix?

_____

_____

_____

Professional women often are granted and use maternity leave and family sick days, and often don't go as far in their careers because of these interruptions to their career paths. Should we grant men paternity leave, and encourage men to equally take on the time commitments necessary for raising the next generation? Why or why not?

_____

_____

_____

The Philosophy

A controversy within feminism concerns how to regard women who choose to adopt traditionally female roles. A truly liberated woman should be free to choose what she wants, but how can we tell whether we are honestly choosing to place family over career, or merely giving in to internalized oppressive prejudices?

Cultural feminism takes a different view of the issue. The central idea is that there really is an essential difference between men and women. Equality shouldn't be about women's ability to do men's work and be considered equal; instead it should be about changing our social values so that women's work and women's virtues are valued as highly as are men's work and men's virtues. In this view, in a male-dominated culture, the values and reward systems of our society have been set up to privilege men, so "women's liberation" in the absence of a change in our values and reward systems just means that women are free to act like men. What if, instead, we changed our society so that raising children, or professions of service and care, were viewed as activities as important and valuable as the stereotypically male pursuits of business and politics—or, at least, changed political and business environments so that they were compatible with and rewarded feminine virtues like collaboration and support rather than masculine virtues of individualistic competition?

An interesting variation of this was brought up by psychiatrist Peter Kramer in his 1993 book *Listening to Prozac*. He asks whether the prevalence of depression among women might be an indication not that many women are mentally ill, but that feminine attributes have been defined as illness. He looks to Victorian feminine ideals—emotional, pensive, moody—and points out that today we'd call these symptoms rather than virtues. What if women are being medicated in order to make them act like men, and to "fit in" better in a male-dominated society?

Of Cyborgs and Goddesses

Identify three things you did because you are female (or, if you are male, because you are male).

1. _____

2. _____

3. _____

You may have been unhappy with that question, but I hope you gave it your best effort. What kinds of considerations did you struggle with in trying to answer the above question?

_____

_____

_____

_____

_____

Given these considerations, when, if ever, does it make sense to say that someone's biological sex determines or even plays a role in their actions and decisions?

_____

_____

_____

_____

The Philosophy

In her famous "Cyborg Manifesto," feminist philosopher Donna Haraway (1944–) tried to put forth a third way, leaving behind this troubling dilemma of how to identify and value some feminine essence. Just arguing for liberation in a patriarchal culture won't work, but trying to recapture and validate a hidden and disrespected feminine nature risks mistaking symptoms of oppression for woman's essential nature. The myth of recapturing your "inner goddess" may be just a way of learning to love your chains. So let's try the idea of a cyborg instead! As she says, "Cyborg imagery can suggest a way out of the maze of dualisms in which we have explained our bodies and our tools to ourselves. . . . Though both are bound in the spiral dance, I would rather be a cyborg than a goddess."

The cyborg has an origin and a nature, but it does not determine her. She is part biology, part technology—nature and nurture—but neither is what she essentially "is." She can make choices about what she becomes; she can change out one part for another. The cyborg doesn't emerge from the Garden, nor is she a Goddess, which implies its own singular (and therefore exclusive) essence. The "truth" of the cyborg's technobiology is found in the military-industrial complex, and this history surely influences, but does not determine what she becomes, as any science fiction story will tell you.

By adopting the image of the cyborg, we can tap into a self-conception that opens up possibilities and leaves room for ambiguities of the kind we all, in fact, experience—of the kind you were asked to explore in these questions. But the role of technology in the image of the cyborg is not just allegorical: Our technologies inform us about who we are, just as do our biology and our culture. Technology has transformed the home, has helped women to free themselves from "women's work," and has allowed "disabled" people to be Olympic athletes. Why not use technology to allow us to transform our nature in order to *become* who we are?

The Lazy Parents

Assuming that we are soon able to do so without discarding "undesirable" fetuses, should we use genetic engineering to ensure that children are no longer born with predispositions to heart disease or to cancer?

_____

_____

_____

_____

What about mental and developmental disabilities? Or just low IQ?

_____

_____

_____

If it is acceptable to use genetic engineering to cure disease, presumably it is because doing so brings about an improved quality of life in our society. Is there any reason not to further improve quality of life by selecting or treating for enhancements, like exceptional health, strength, or intelligence?

_____

_____

_____

The Philosophy

Eugenics has become a dirty word, and for very good reasons. In the past, the idea of "improving" the human gene pool has been a screen for racism, and has been used as a justification for programs of forced sterilization in Nazi Germany and in the United States. Some contemporary bioethicists, however, have raised the possibility of a "liberal eugenics" that doesn't allow for these reprehensible possibilities. A liberal eugenics would not force any participation, but would simply allow parents to make genetic choices about their own offspring. Elimination of undesirable characteristics would be done by opting in on an individual basis rather than by excluding certain people from having children, so nobody's rights would be infringed upon, and there's no possibility of takeover by a racist or political agenda.

There are clear advantages to genetic engineering. There are a great many genetic disorders that cause suffering and death, and these could be avoided. But once we open the door to curing genetic disease, the question of genetic enhancement arises. Bioethicist and Oxford professor Julian Savulescu (1963–) argues that not only is it acceptable to choose to enhance our children, it would in fact be wrong not to. He asks us to consider "the case of the Neglectful Parents." They have an exceptionally intelligent child who needs a cheap, easy-to-find dietary supplement to maintain her intellect, but they don't bother with it, and she becomes normal. We would say these parents have been irresponsible, and have wronged their child. Now consider another case: "the Lazy Parents." They have a normal child, but there's a new, cheap, easy-to-find dietary supplement that gives normal children an exceptional intellect— but they don't bother with it. Isn't this just as wrong? If so, then wouldn't it be wrong of us not to make our children exceptional once genetic engineering technologies are advanced enough to allow us to do so? If we have an obligation to maintain a benefit, why don't we have an obligation to create one?

The New Breed

Here are a series of troubling questions adapted from bioethicist John Harris's Wonderwoman and Superman: The Ethics of Human Biotechnology. *First, come up with a list of things you think are important genetic issues (maybe disorders, heart conditions, depressive disposition, etc.), and a list of things you think are trivial matters of genetic choice (maybe hair color, height, cheeriness, etc.).*

Important:

_____

Trivial:

_____

Of the important issues: if they are important, why leave them to chance? Of the trivial issues: if they are trivial, why not let parents decide?

_____

_____

_____

This seems to justify allowing parents full freedom to make all attributes of children available to parents' choices. What kind of society would result from allowing parents to enhance their children in whatever ways and to whatever extent they can?

_____

_____

_____

The Philosophy

A problem with the idea of liberal eugenics is that, although we might be able to say that the opt-in structure means that nobody is being forced to participate, there are widespread social effects that we can expect to emerge from those individual choices. Just as we saw with Economic Justice, when we look at individual rights alone (property rights in one case, choosing for your kids in the other) we risk missing important things in the big picture (economic inequality in one case, and in this case social-biological inequality).

These technologies will presumably be quite expensive at first, at the very least. This means that a liberal approach will allow economic inequalities to create genetic inequalities, giving the children of the wealthy an even greater set of advantages in our society. Now, equal opportunity doesn't mean equal outcomes, and economic inequality already creates biological inequality—lead poisoning and nutritional deficiencies, for example, have lifelong consequences and affect the poor *much* more so than the rich—but surely liberal eugenics would further expand the opportunities and advantages of the wealthy over the disadvantaged.

There's also a problem of coercion. If genetic enhancement becomes cheap enough to be widespread, those who might choose to have a "natural" child would be, in effect, giving their child a disability. How are they supposed to compete with what John Harris called "The New Breed"? What if some physical trait showed that they were of the "old breed"—for example, a slight asymmetry of the face? Would employers hire them when an enhanced "new breed" candidate was also applying for the position?

But then, what's the alternative? Only allow enhancements once we can governmentally subsidize them, so they are equally available to all? Put genetic choice off limits, and allow people to suffer and die from preventable genetic conditions?

CHAPTER 7

---
*

Aspects
of the Self

In this chapter we turn to an assortment of different questions of the will and of the self—questions of choice, responsibility, and of what sort of thing there is within us that can make choices, have responsibility, or can even "have" experiences in the first place. All this touches on some religious and some biological issues as well. Looking at the mind naturally brings up questions of the mind's relation to the brain and to human evolution; it also brings up questions of the mind's relation to the soul and our possible fate after death. As in previous chapters, the questions here may require you to play along with some assumptions. By turns, I'll ask you to adopt, at least temporarily, assumptions of the evolutionary origin of the species, Judeo-Christian assumptions about God and sin, and assumptions of reincarnation from Asian religions.

Things are going to get pretty crazy by the end of this chapter. Have fun!

Why Minds?

Do you believe in the freedom of the will? Why?

_____

_____

_____

_____

_____

_____

What would your experience be like if we don't have free will? Would you be able to tell?

_____

_____

_____

_____

_____

_____

The Philosophy

William James (1842–1910), an American Pragmatist philosopher and psychologist, considered the idea of *epiphenomenalism*—the idea that mental events, like thoughts, experiences, and intentions, are merely secondary effects that play no causal role. If this is true, all our decisions are made through unconscious processes, and conscious experience just hangs around making up explanations after the fact. The epiphenomenalist believes that mental experiences are like the smoke rising from a train: They are only a byproduct that is produced along the way. All the real work happens down below.

There's something to be said for the view. Sometimes, when we are startled—as, for example, when hearing a sudden noise while walking through the woods at night—we react first and only find that we have the experience of fright once we have already begun to run away. James claims, though, that evolutionary biology indicates this view must be wrong. Surely, whatever you think about whether and which animals have minds and mental experiences, if you go back far enough in evolutionary history there must have been a time when no such things existed. So consciousness and thought evolved at some point, along with the nervous system. If consciousness plays no role in determining our actions, why would these things have come into being? In what way could they be evolutionarily adaptive, unless they are part of a feedback loop: Our consciousness is stimulated by the environment and, in turn, plays a role in determining our actions in that environment?

And yet couldn't it be that the feedback loop is adaptive and effective, but our consciousness of it is still just an aftereffect? But if this is the case, then why wouldn't we simply have brains, but not minds?

Vertigo

Most people believe we have a free will, but our choices are conditioned by circumstances, history, mood, and a variety of other factors. It's best not to go grocery shopping while you're hungry, for example. How can you tell when your choice is under some influence or another?

It's not easy, is it? Even when we aren't choosing entirely freely, we feel as if we are—at least while we're making the choice. But aren't there some circumstances in which you aren't just influenced in your decisions, but really aren't responsible for your actions?

If you said, "Yes," isn't it still true that you could have chosen otherwise in these "determined" circumstances? Isn't your will always basically free, then?

The Philosophy

The French existentialist Jean-Paul Sartre (1905–1980) explored our experience of radical freedom in a variety of different ways. As a quick demonstration that we experience our will as entirely and radically free, he presented the experience of vertigo. Try this yourself, next time you're a few stories up or near a cliff or something; you'll see that he's right.

Sartre says that the experience of vertigo is not a fear of falling. The feeling is one of excited agitation, not fear, and the experience is not notably more intense when there's a real risk of slipping and falling (although then we may indeed experience fear in addition to vertigo). The experience of vertigo, instead, is the awareness that at the next moment we may choose to throw ourselves over the edge. It's not that we want to, even secretly or subconsciously. It's that, even though every fiber of our being shouts "No!" we are still aware that in the very next moment we could suddenly decide otherwise and that our current resolve does nothing to diminish our freedom in the next moment.

Along the same lines, he asks us to consider the gambler (although any kind of addict works equally well). The gambler may choose with full resolve not to gamble, but as soon as the question comes up again—perhaps friends are getting together for cards, or there's merely an idle hour in the day and a casino nearby—that previous resolve counts for nothing. He must decide again, starting from scratch, every day and every moment that the question presents itself.

In this way, at the very least, we see that we always experience ourselves as possessed of a radical freedom; not only able, but condemned to choose.

Divine Foreknowledge

If you have free will, does God know what you will choose?

_____

_____

_____

_____

If God doesn't know what you'll choose, why not, if God is omniscient and omnipotent? If God does know what you'll choose, why does He let you choose to do bad things?

_____

_____

_____

If God lets you do bad things, when He could have stopped you, is it fair to punish you for doing what He could have stopped? Or, if it's fair to punish you for your intention alone, why not stop you from doing something and just punish you for what you would have done?

_____

_____

_____

The Philosophy

St. Anselm of Canterbury (1033–1109) took up the issue of divine foreknowledge and its seeming conflict with free will, and it really is a serious problem, if you think about it. If God is omniscient, it seems as if God must know what we are going to do before we do it. But if God knows what we're going to do before we do it, then there must be some knowable fact about what we are going to do, and that fact must exist before we do it. But if there's a fact about what we're going to do before we do it, then we don't choose freely, because there's already a fact about what we will have chosen while we are choosing to do it. That seems to mean that we couldn't have chosen otherwise; therefore, we don't have free will. If we don't have free will, then we're not responsible for our actions, in which case surely it's wrong to judge us on what we do. Which is to say that God's judgment must be unjust.

Did you get all that? Do you see the problem? It's weird stuff, but it makes sense once you're in the middle of it.

The issue was actually explored brilliantly in "Minority Report," a short story about "precrime" written by Philip K. Dick (1928–1982) in the 1950s. (You may be more familiar with the film *Minority Report*, which is less brilliant, but contains significantly more chase scenes, for whatever that's worth.) How can there be free will if there's foreknowledge of choices that will be made? And how can punishment for predetermined crimes be justified?

Anselm's solution is very elegant. He claimed that the confusion is created by the false assumption that God exists in time. God, he says, exists outside of time itself, and so He sees all times as if they were present at once. The progress of time moves forward and the future is always open, and yet God can see the future even though (from our perspective, *in* time) the future doesn't even exist and is entirely undetermined.

Moral Choice and Divine Punishment

One traditional response to the Problem of Evil (previously discussed in the chapter on God) is that God has to allow evil in order to let us have free will. Why would free will be so important to God?

_____

_____

_____

_____

Why not just let us choose freely, but have our bad actions always happen to fail?

_____

_____

_____

_____

Couldn't we get the value of learning to make good rather than bad choices by just having free will when there's not too much at stake? Like we could choose to lie and cheat, but it would never occur to us to murder?

_____

_____

_____

The Philosophy

It makes some immediate sense to think that God would want us to choose to do the right thing—for us to have the option to do otherwise, but to do the good because we know and value the goodness of the good. But couldn't God create us with the knowledge of good already? Maybe we only truly understand something when we learn it through experience, because we are of necessity not infinite beings, and so our reason and understanding is finite. And, additionally, we need to be responsible for our choices if God is going to judge us, and we don't deserve praise for doing the right thing unless we could have done otherwise.

Of course, we might wish to ask why God chose to create a bunch of flawed beings that can make choices so that God can judge them. What's the value in judging? But maybe the point isn't the judging, but the understanding of the good—but if this is the case, it seems as if God should value those humans who "get it," but not eternally punish those who don't. What's the point of the punishment?

It could be that free will in moral choices wasn't God's plan, but is the result of eating the fruit of the Tree of Knowledge, the original sin that lays the ground for punishment if we fail to become good. But shouldn't God have known that Adam would eat the apple? God starts to sound like an abusive parent: "Now look what you made me do!"

Søren Kierkegaard, whose ideas about Abraham we discussed in the chapter on God, has an interesting view on Adam's choice. He considered that Adam had never known suffering or evil and could have had no idea of what a "consequence" would be. How could he have made the choice of whether or not to eat the apple when he had never experienced anything bad and did not know right from wrong? This experience of anxiety (or, in Kierkegaard's Danish, *angst*) characterizes many of our choices today: It is the uncertainty of actions where we know the meaning of our choices will only emerge after we have made them.

The Responsibility of Objects

It's often said that "Guns don't kill people; people kill people." Literally, this is obviously true. Objects don't do things. But the phrase is supposed to be a response to a position that isn't so obviously false. What's the position this phrase is responding to, and what kind of responsibility does the gun bear according to that position?

_____

_____

_____

It is clear in some cases that the things around us influence our choices. For example, if fast-food restaurants are required to put calorie counts on their menus, customers make healthier choices. How much responsibility does the restaurant menu's information or lack of information bear, and how much responsibility does the customer bear in either case?

_____

_____

_____

Organ donation rates rise if people getting driver's licenses are asked if they'd like to be donors, rather than leaving it to them to seek out and check the box on the application form. What does this say about responsibility and influence?

_____

_____

The Philosophy

The argument about the gun's responsibility in gun violence might seem intractable, but there's good reason to think that it isn't. Once we separate *responsibility* from *blame*, things get much simpler. The Actor-Network Theory of Bruno Latour (1947–), a contemporary French sociologist of science and technology, can help explain.

Latour talks about "scripts" that go along with the objects around us. The gun carries with it a series of intentions and scenarios, because guns do certain things and not others. This lays out certain pathways, which "translate" our goals and intentions. We end up thinking about ourselves and our possible interactions differently when we're holding guns, even concealed weapons. Now, this doesn't mean that the gun *determines* what we will do, but that it provides a context for action that would be inappropriate to ignore. As Latour puts it, although the agent may have intentions and goals, the gun has its script, and when the agent has a gun we can't consider either the agent or the gun in isolation, but we have to look at the intentions of the agent-gun network.

Doesn't this make it seem as if the "gun" has an intention? Isn't that just crazy? Understood literally, it would be, but the gun *does* carry with it a series of intentions. The script of the gun gives us a series of roles to play, and it is easy to assume and play out those roles, not unlike how water flows into a riverbed rather than over the banks.

This can help us see the responsibility that things bear in our decision making, and you can see how the same analysis applies to the other examples discussed previously. But all this has left aside the question of blame!— and rightly so. We know full well that we make decisions in situations that influence choice, but that those situations clearly do not *make* us choose one thing rather than another. Not everyone with a gun makes the choice to shoot. Simply blaming the gun is wrong, as is simply blaming a person without considering the circumstances of choice.

Heart and Soul

Do you believe that there is a soul that survives death? What's the basis for your belief?

_____

_____

_____

_____

_____

_____

What kind of thing is a thought? Where do thoughts come from, and what are they made of?

_____

_____

_____

_____

_____

_____

The Philosophy

In his *Meditations on First Philosophy*, French philosopher René Descartes gave an argument that he thought showed that the mind is separate from the body and that it survives death. The body, he pointed out, is "extended" (that is, it exists in space, has length and volume, and so on), but does not think. The mind, on the other hand, does think but is not extended. He thinks these characteristics can be easily verified through introspection. Consider a thought—where is it? How many cups of water would it hold if you hollowed it out? Imagine cutting it in half: What is half a thought like? How many would you need to make a coat? The other side of the matter seems clear enough as well. We're made of meat and bone, and only a brief conversation with a steak should be enough to convince you that there's not a lot going on in there.

If the mind is thinking and not extended, and the body is extended and not thinking, then they seem to be entirely distinct and separable. So the mind's survival upon the body's death is at least possible. But, further, can there be something like half a mind? Of course not; the mind doesn't have parts—and so, Descartes argues, it cannot decay, and must therefore be eternal. So there you go: proof of the eternal soul!

The argument is pretty silly, of course. Just because things appear to us to be a certain way doesn't make it so. It's true today as it was then that we don't really understand the connection between the brain as physical matter and the mind as we experience it "from the inside," but we have plenty of evidence that damage to the one affects the other, and today we're more likely to think that thoughts are "emergent phenomena"—not really *things* at all, but something more like processes that we call things for convenience.

Other Minds

What if what was called "red" was experienced as red by you but was experienced as green by others? Is there any way you could tell?

_____

_____

_____

_____

What if what you experienced as pain was experienced as soothing by others, and they just happen to enjoy pain and dislike being soothed? Is there any way you could tell?

_____

_____

_____

_____

What if some other people aren't conscious and don't have thoughts but are just very complicated biological mechanisms without a will or inner experiences? Is there any way you could tell?

_____

_____

_____

_____

The Philosophy

As far as I know, Descartes was the first to bring up this kind of question, and it makes sense that it would have arisen in the seventeenth century. At that time, automata, or self-moving machines, were a popular amusement among the wealthy—for example, when someone stepped on a switch hidden in a garden path a nude statue by the side of the path would turn to cover itself. Descartes asked his reader to imagine looking outside a window: We say that we see people going by, when in fact the senses only tell us that we see umbrellas and coats, which could as easily be a series of dressed up automata passing by. Reason, not our senses, tells us that they are people.

Now, Descartes's point was just about how we know what we know—whether from reason or from the senses. The more radical question is how we can be sure that there's an "inside" inside of other people at all. The most popular answer has been that we know this by analogy. We act a certain way, and mental experiences accompany those actions, so it stands to reason that others have similar mental experiences when they act in similar ways.

We can supplement this with some biological considerations. We know that colors, for example, correspond to different wavelengths of light and that our eyes and brains are constituted in definable and functionally equivalent ways, and this supports the idea that the experience of light with a wavelength around 700 nm should be not only consistently *called* red, but also consistently *experienced* as red.

The uncertainty of this, though, is still troubling. The what-it's-like, or *qualia*, of a physical experience seems unrelated to the physical basis. There's no "redness" in the wavelength, or in the eye, or in the synapses of the brain. Similarly, although there may be physical phenomena in the brain associated with the experience of pain, there's nothing painlike to be found there—and consciousness itself isn't something we can point to either.

Continuity of Self

What if you were a different person yesterday? Is it possible that the yesterday-you died, and you came into being this morning and just inherited yesterday-you's memories?

_____

_____

_____

_____

Is it possible that there are two of you right now, but you're unaware of each other, and you simply share the same memories as if you had each experienced them?

_____

_____

_____

_____

Is it possible that, five minutes ago, you switched bodies and memories with someone else? If you're out in public, look to your right. Could you have been that person just a few minutes ago?

_____

_____

_____

_____

The Philosophy

The English philosopher John Locke (1632–1704) considered these questions, and his answer might be summarized as, "Sure, why not?" We have no way of knowing that each of us is a single self, or that we are the same selves that we were. The only clue we have about whether the self is constant over time is continuity of consciousness, and—past the present moment—that boils down to memory. But rather than concluding that all of these things are possible, Locke's take-away point was that what we *mean* by "the self" and by personal identity *is* this continuity of consciousness. So if you remember being yesterday-you, then it doesn't really make sense to even ask whether yesterday-you might have died, to be replaced by today-you (or, in other words, *you*-you). What you mean by saying that that was you yesterday is nothing else but that yesterday-you's experiences belong to you as yours.

Locke gives a few more examples to show that it is consciousness that makes us who we are, not some underlying substance. If you lose a hand, there is no question that you continue to be the same person. If, on the other hand (so to speak), consciousness were located in our little fingers, if the finger were severed, we would rightly say that the finger remains the person no matter what happens to the rest of the body. Locke also considers the soul of a prince suddenly entering the body of a cobbler; today, instead, we might imagine a two-direction brain transplant. If consciousness and memory are continuous from the old bodies to the new ones, surely we'd say that the persons switched bodies, not that the persons switched brains.

Is the Self a Thing?

We were just considering whether the yesterday-you is the same you as the today-you. What does that even mean? What is the "you" that has your experiences?

_____

_____

_____

_____

Have you ever had an experience of your "you," or just experiences of perceptions and ideas that you experienced as "yours"?

_____

_____

_____

_____

If yesterday-you might not be the same as today-you, is there any reason why you should care whether you-you dies tonight in your sleep, to be replaced by another "you" (who isn't you) tomorrow?

_____

_____

_____

_____

The Philosophy

For Scottish philosopher David Hume (1711–1776), all of these questions would have been a load of crap. To even think that they make sense, you have to make a big metaphysical assumption: that there is some kind of permanent "self" that "has" experiences and hangs around behind the scenes through your whole life. But what basis is there for such a belief? We don't have any experience of a self at all. Sure, everything we experience is experienced as *our* experience, but we don't have any experience of being a thing that *has* those experiences—we only experience the experiences. "The mind," Hume wrote, "is a kind of theatre, where several perceptions successively make their appearance." But even this analogy is flawed, because it implies at least a constant *stage* upon which these experiences appear. Hume added that "the comparison of the theatre must not mislead us. They are the successive perceptions only, that constitute the mind; nor have we the most distant notion of the place, where these scenes are represented, or of the materials, of which it is compos'd."

Hume had no patience for things we would like to believe, if there is no evidence to support them, and this is abundantly clear in this case. What else could we believe more strongly than that we exist as subjects—as things to which our experiences *happen*? And yet our experience is entirely and precisely devoid of any experience of the self: When we try to imagine the self that undergoes an experience, we find that is has no qualities or attributes apart from the experience it is undergoing. Worse yet, when we try to contemplate the "self" having the experience, we find that the self has already retreated! Try it—you'll find that you are no longer the you having the experience. Instead you've become the you that is experiencing contemplating the "you" that had had the experience. And now that you're thinking about *that*, you're another step removed (and now, another [and now, another (and so on)]).

Life of the Will and Death of the Self

Do you believe in any kind of reincarnation or transmigration of souls? If so, what kind, and why?

_____

_____

_____

_____

Most people don't have memories of past lives, so it seems that if any kind of transmigration occurs, it usually includes memory loss. But if memories are lost, what is it, exactly, that is transferred?

_____

_____

_____

_____

Assume for the moment that after your death you will become someone else but have no memory of having been who you are today. Why would you care? Would that be any different to you than if you were entirely annihilated rather than reborn?

_____

_____

_____

The Philosophy

In the nineteenth century, philosophical works from Asia were becoming available to Europeans, and Arthur Schopenhauer developed a post-Kantian view of the world very much in keeping with the German tradition but strongly influenced by Buddhism and by the Hindu *Vedas*. He thought that just as we ourselves appear in two aspects—to the senses and to science we appear as a thing, but in our inner experience we experience ourselves as thought and will—so too is everything in reality both matter and will. Will is the "inner truth" and reality of the world. The will, then, is not destroyed by death. Will continues on in the soil that our bodies become, in the plants that that soil becomes as they take up its nutrients, and in the animals that those plants become as the plants are eaten and digested, and so on. Individuality dies, but the will is indestructible.

Schopenhauer presented this in a dialogue, where he imagined the anguished reply, "I—I—*I* want to exist! That is what I care about, and not an existence which has to be reasoned out first in order to show that it is mine." This, Schopenhauer thinks, is ridiculous. The "I" of the will, the "subject" that undergoes experiences and wills to live, is the *least* distinctive and individual thing about us! The will to live drives us as it drives all things, even against our own interests and happiness! The will traps us in an unending cycle of desire, and life becomes nothing but the constant cycle from the pain of desire to the boredom of satisfaction. We should seek instead, not that the "I" should survive death, but that the "I" should be destroyed within life—in a Buddhistic "negation of the will." Even death does not quiet the will. Only ceasing the cycle of desire can free us from the will and from suffering.

✳

CHAPTER 8

Knowledge
and Reality

There are a wealth of different philosophical issues having to do with what's real and how (and whether) we can know about it. Many of these questions appear in the other chapters—questions of knowledge and reality are at the base of most of the questions in this book. In this chapter, though, we look at questions having to do specifically with what knowledge is, and how it connects us or fails to connect us with reality outside of the mind.

If you have some philosophical training, you may be disappointed that we're passing over some major issues. Some topics within questions of knowledge and reality, though very important within academic philosophy today, are too technical and deeply embedded with the history and context of scholarly argumentation to present well in a short, concise form. It's also difficult to ask interesting questions about those topics, especially for readers who might not have much background. So I've left out some worthy topics, to be sure, but this selection will give you a good sense of how philosophers talk about these issues, and should provide a good basis for some interesting conversations!

The Stuff of Stuff

There's a bunch of stuff everywhere, right? What's it made of? And what is that stuff made of? Is there some basic stuff that all other stuff is made of? If so, what's it made of?

_____

_____

_____

Some stuff sometimes becomes other stuff—like how ice melts. When stuff becomes other stuff, is it still the same stuff? If it is, then why isn't it the same anymore? If it isn't, then what happened—did some stuff get added or taken away from the other stuff?

_____

_____

_____

All this stuff got here from somewhere—presumably from other stuff, because stuff doesn't just show up; stuff is made out of stuff. How did all this different stuff end up being so different? Is all this stuff really different stuff? Mustn't it be that all this different stuff is really the same, because it's all made out of the same stuff?

_____

_____

_____

The Philosophy

Have you ever noticed how if you keep saying the same word over and over again, it starts to seem really weird? "Is that how that word is spelled?" "What does that word mean exactly?" This is what's called *semantic saturation*, and the same thing happens when you think about an idea for long enough. "Stuff" is a weird word, but it's not nearly as weird as stuff itself is, when you think about it long enough.

The ancient Greek philosopher Thales (c. 624–c. 546 B.C.E.) is often called the first philosopher in the entire European tradition, and his main idea was that everything is made out of water. Now you're probably thinking, *Water?* Actually, it's not nearly as stupid as it sounds. Things undergo change, so there must be some *underlying* thing that things are made from that is the thing that undergoes the change. Things don't just appear and disappear. As to what that underlying thing is, water is actually a pretty good candidate. We can see how water changes into ice or into steam. Water is taken up by plants, and becomes their leaves and fruit, and it replenishes our bodies as well.

Other philosophers around the same time—often called "the Presocratics" because they were mostly working before Socrates was around—had different theories. Anaximander (c. 610–c. 546 B.C.E.) said the stuff was undefined, but became different stuff through heat, cold, moisture, and dryness. Pythagoras (c. 570–c. 495 B.C.E.) thought the basis of the world was mathematical. Heraclitus (c. 535–c. 475 B.C.E.) said everything was fire, but he might have meant that metaphorically—fire is a process, not a thing, and he said that the only constant unchanging thing in the world was change itself. Parmenides (c. 515–c. 450 B.C.E.) went the other direction and said change is an illusion and there is only a single unchanging thing. Democritus (c. 460–c. 370 B.C.E.) even claimed that the world was really made of tiny indivisible things (the Greek word is *atom*) that combine in different forms to make things. Crazy, right?

The Problem of Induction

How does gravity work? Don't use technical terms to fill in the gaps—try to really explain it.

_____

_____

_____

_____

We all know that gravity works, at least. Could mass start to repel itself instead of attracting itself, as of tomorrow? Is there anything any less likely about repelling than attracting, or anything about "mass" that makes it make more sense somehow that it would attract other mass rather than repel it?

_____

_____

_____

_____

Why couldn't the laws of nature change suddenly? Is there a law of nature that the laws of nature can't change? Why can't that law change? Is there a law that the law that the laws of nature can't change can't change?

_____

_____

_____

_____

The Philosophy

These are questions that Scottish philosopher David Hume brought up in what has come to be known as his "problem of induction." Induction—the process by which we use particular instances to demonstrate a general rule—seemed to him to be suspicious in a very basic way. How many cases are enough to establish that things will *always* and *necessarily* work a certain way? Assume some number of cases, n, is enough. What did the nth case have that the $n-1$ case didn't? Wouldn't we, instead, need an infinite number of cases to show that it will *always* and *necessarily* work out that way?

Worse yet, the very idea of using different cases (for example, that you drop stuff and it falls) to establish a "law" (e.g., gravity) is dependent on the idea that nature is consistent—that the future will be like the past. If the future isn't like the past, then past evidence doesn't have any predictive value at all. But what evidence do we have that the future will be like the past? The only evidence is that *in the past* the future

has always been like the past, so it seems like *in the future* the future will also be like the past. But this is question-begging circular reasoning—the only evidence we have depends on simply *assuming* what it is supposed to be evidence for!

And we also have no recourse to just *seeing* these connections between events. There's nothing "drowninglike" about water—the only way to find out that it can't be breathed is the hard way. Same thing with the coldness of ice, or the saltiness of salt, or the "fallingness" of things heavier than air. If these causal structures had a logical basis, then we could know that they will always and necessarily be that way, but because we only find out these connections through experience, we can only make claims about them through inductive reasoning. Which, according to the arguments we just went through, seems arbitrary and unjustified. So about knowledge and certainty about nature and cause and effect?—forget it.

Everything You Believe about the World Is Wrong

Imagine anything—a stick, maybe. It has a length. Imagine cutting it in half. Now again. Now again. And so on. Can you keep dividing it in half infinitely? If so, doesn't that mean it isn't made of anything?

_____

_____

_____

Okay, so that's a problem, right? There must be a point when you can't divide it in half anymore. That indivisible thing: does it have length? If it does, then you can divide it in half, right? But if it doesn't, then it's not a thing, right? What's going on?

_____

_____

_____

Okay, how about this: Does the universe have a beginning? If so, something must have started it, so you're not at the beginning yet. But then what started the starting? And what started that? On the other hand, if it doesn't have a beginning, how can it exist? A series of events can't have started without having a start, right? Right?

_____

_____

_____

The Philosophy

Immanuel Kant, inspired by the deeply troubling problems about knowledge brought up by David Hume, wrote his monumental *Critique of Pure Reason*, in which he tried to show what kinds of things are within the realm of human knowledge, and what kinds of things aren't. To get at this, he first identified the structures that allow us to think and perceive things at all—including forms of the senses (space and time) and categories of the understanding (including "substance" and "cause"). These structures make experience *possible*, and so there is literally no possible way we can know if they're true—if we saw something that didn't exist in space, we'd either experience it as if it did, or we wouldn't experience it at all, because the ideas of "seeing" and "thing" only make sense at all *in the form of space*.

And consider this: How did you learn that space and time are empty and infinite, that the first has three dimensions and the second has only one? There's no way you could have learned that; you've never had an experience of *just* space, or empty time. These are structures that make experience possible, not things outside of the mind.

That's why when we ask about the beginning of time or what things are made of, we get into problems like the ones in the questions you just answered. Reason tells us that the universe must have a beginning, but that it also can't possibly have one (because what happened before then?), and that things must be made of stuff, but that all stuff can be divided (and then it's not made of anything in the end!). The problem here is that we're using structures of human understanding (space, time, substance, causality) and we're pretending that they're *really real*, not just for human experience, but *in reality*.

So, we can't show that these things are real because if they were false, we'd never know. And if we assume they're real, we run into serious logical contradictions. So the conclusion should be this: Whatever is real, it's not anything like what makes sense to us.

Agrippa's Trilemma

Assume for a moment that you know something. Anything at all. If you know it to be true, there must be some reason why. But you have to know that reason too, so there must be a reason you know that reason to be true. And so on. Can't we just keep asking "But why?" over and over again?

Is it possible that there are some things that we know, but which we don't need to give reasons for? Some things that are self-justifying?

If there aren't some self-justifying "foundational" things that we know, can we really know anything? We can't just keep giving reasons infinitely—there has to be some sort of basis, right?

The Philosophy

This argument has been around since the ancient Greeks, and is sometimes called "Agrippa's Trilemma." Put most directly, it goes like this:

Premise 1: You know something.
Premise 2: Knowledge requires justification.
Premise 3: Nothing can be its own justification.

Conclusion: Knowledge requires an infinite series of justifications, which is impossible, and contradicts the first premise.

So, either we accept the conclusion that knowledge is impossible and deny the first premise, or we deny the second premise by claiming that some forms of knowledge don't require reasons at all, or we deny the third premise and say that some forms of knowledge can be evidence for themselves.

Philosophers have pursued all three options. The first is the position of the skep-tic. The second is the position of "foundationalism," which claims that some things can be "the end of the line" in reason giving. Usually, the foundations given are sense data, but Descartes tried the foundation of self-knowledge. "I exist" doesn't need a justification, in his view, because as soon as we doubt it, we find that we are there, doing the doubting! But getting from "I think, therefore I am" to any knowledge about anything else is, well, hard to argue convincingly. The third option is "coherentism," which is the view that there are no foundational beliefs, and no ends to the process of giving reasons, but that it's okay for reason giving to be circular. On this view, the coherence of a big set of beliefs gives all of them a collective justification. So you might not be able to prove that you're not asleep and dreaming right now, but the coherence of the different views that support that idea gives you reason enough to say you know you're awake.

Justified True Belief

A commonsense definition of "knowledge" is that it is a belief that is justified and true. Does this make sense? Can you think of things rightly called "knowledge" that are false or unjustified?

_____

_____

_____

_____

Imagine that you see what appears to be a sheep in a field, and claim to know that there is a sheep in the field. Now, it turns out that what you saw was a dog in a sheep outfit, but that there is a sheep in the field; it's on the other side of a hill, where you can't see it. Your belief was justified, and true, but would you call it knowledge?

_____

_____

_____

_____

_____

The Philosophy

Problems like this are called "Gettier cases," after Edmund Gettier's (1927–) 1963 article, "Is Justified True Belief Knowledge?" Gettier's original cases seem a little silly to me, although they do effectively demonstrate a problem. In one of them, we imagine that Smith has good reason to believe that Jones owns a Ford, and so Smith claims to know that "either Jones owns a Ford, or Brown is in Barcelona," while having no idea where Brown is. Now, even though Smith was justified in thinking that Jones owns a Ford, this happens to be wrong. But as it happens, Brown *is* in Barcelona, although Smith had no reason to think so. And so Smith's claim is justified, and is true, but we're not likely to say that he *knew* it. The sheep example in Question 2 is from Roderick Chisholm (1916–1999) and works basically the same way.

Philosophers have responded to the Gettier problem in a great number of different ways. Maybe we need to say that the justification of a belief needs to be connected in some way with its truth—for example, the justification of these beliefs (looking at the dressed-up dog, or having reason to believe Jones owns a Ford) is there, but it's disconnected from the fact of the matter that makes the belief true (the hidden sheep over the hill, or Brown's whereabouts).

We might say instead that in addition to the truth of the thing we claim to know, the evidence that forms the basis of justification must itself be true. A valuable kind of question might be this: If the thing that we claim to know were false, would that affect our belief in it? In these cases, if the sheep were in the woods or if Brown were in Boston, the justification would still be there, and the belief as well, but the belief would be false—so this shows that the justification of the belief isn't "hooked up" properly with the facts that make the belief true.

The Ethics of Belief

Imagine a ship owner who hasn't taken the boat into dry dock for maintenance for some time. He worries whether the ship is in good condition but convinces himself to have faith. He rents the ship to some emigrants; it sinks and kills those aboard. Is the ship owner right to have an untroubled conscience, because he firmly believed (without sufficient evidence) that the ship was safe?

_____

_____

_____

_____

_____

What do you have faith in? Could any of these elements of your beliefs bring harm to others, or diminish their rights and freedoms? For example: that God doesn't equally respect gay marriage, or that abortion is permissible because the fetus isn't a person, or that abortion is immoral because the fetus is a person, or that assisted suicide is always wrong. How can you be responsible in acting on these beliefs?

_____

_____

_____

_____

The Philosophy

The case of the ship owner comes from English philosopher W. K. Clifford (1845–1879), who used it as the starting point of his famous essay, "The Ethics of Belief." Clifford argued that it is always wrong to hold beliefs in the absence of sufficient evidence in their favor; similarly, it is always wrong to ignore evidence that goes against our beliefs. We can't just have faith in things, because our beliefs begin to affect others as soon as we act on them, and therefore we have a responsibility to those around us to form our beliefs in a responsible manner and to maintain their justification by calling them into question whenever we have reason to.

This process—epistemic responsibility—is pretty difficult. Like the ship owner, we are too easily seduced by self-interest into disregarding "inconvenient truths." What's more, we often fail to notice evidence contrary to our beliefs because of confirmation bias, which makes us focus instead on the evidence that fits with what we already believe.

Here's an example that shows how easily our attention brings us to bad beliefs. Imagine you've got 100 employees, and ten of them are stealing from your business. You give them all a polygraph test, which is 90 percent accurate. How likely are you to correctly identify the thieves? Stop reading here, think about it for a minute, and settle on an answer.

Okay, you're back. You said 90 percent likely, right? Chances are you did. That's because you were focused on the ten thieves, and you forgot about the ninety innocents. If the test is 90 percent accurate, you'll correctly identify nine of the thieves. But the test is also wrong 10 percent of the time, so you'll falsely accuse nine of the ninety innocents. So the test will identify eighteen people as guilty, with only a 50 percent rate of correct identification.

This is but one example of how quickly things like focus, self-interest, and confirmation bias can make epistemic responsibility difficult. Within the realm of religious belief, where contrary evidence can't be found at all, the problem of responsibility in acting on your beliefs seems even more difficult—at least in those cases where your beliefs may bring harm to others.

Bullshit, and the Bullshitting Bullshitters That Bullshit

Harry Frankfurt (1929–), a contemporary American philosopher, claims that "One of the most salient features of our culture is that there is so much bullshit. Everyone knows this." How would you characterize bullshitting—how is it, for example, different from lying?

_____

_____

_____

_____

Arguably, the two domains where bullshit is most prevalent are in marketing and in politics (which seem to have more and more in common). What effect does the mountain of bullshit in marketing have on our economy?

_____

_____

_____

What about the mountain of bullshit in our politics—what effect does this have on our democracy?

_____

_____

_____

The Philosophy

Frankfurt explored the phenomenon of bullshit in an essay, appropriately titled "On Bullshit," which has since been published as a little stand-alone book. He's obviously quite right to identify bullshit as a significant aspect of our society, worthy of careful consideration, although there are perhaps some obvious reasons why the topic hadn't been written about too much before he took it up.

In Frankfurt's analysis, bullshit is characterized by a lack of concern for the truth. In lies, there is a matter of fact that the liar is concerned with, even if that concern is limited to covering it up. The bullshitter, by contrast, is not concerned with covering over the truth about some matter of fact; rather, he wants to cover over the truth about his own *intention* in speaking. The bullshitter may in fact say things that are true, but he doesn't say them because he cares about whether they are true or false. For example, Frankfurt considers a politician giving a Fourth of July speech. He may say a lot of nice things about liberty and founding principles and whatever, some of which may be true, or even insightful, but the speaker's concern is not with history or political philosophy—the speaker's concern is that he is viewed as someone who cares about all that stuff. To give an example from advertising, consider the claims "100% Natural" or "Contains a clinically tested ingredient." Both may be true, but that doesn't mean they aren't bullshit.

We see this pretty clearly in student writing. Surely you've written some bullshit at some point. Student bullshitting consists largely of vague claims that could well be true, but which are directed at *taking up space* and *sounding on topic* rather than actually providing information or analysis. Information and analysis, after all, can be identified as wrong, which will lose points on the assignment. Student bullshitting seeks to finish out the assignment while providing as little to grasp onto as possible . . . not unlike much political rhetoric.

CHAPTER 9

✳

Science

There's a great deal at stake for us in questions of the meaning, structure, and importance of science, and a great many of these questions are much thornier and troubling than most of us appreciate. Science is something of a given for us today—we believe in the certainty of its claims, and in the consistent forward progress of scientific knowledge—but when pressed on how science works or the concept of science itself, what makes science scientific, it slips easily through our fingers.

I should make a preliminary note about Martin Heidegger (1889–1976), who will show up at the end of this chapter. Unlike the other German philosophers whom we have discussed or will discuss who were adults and living in Germany during the rise of Nazism, Heidegger did not flee the country, and actually became a member of the Nazi party. Later in life, he claimed that he soon realized that this had been a mistake; he also said that he criticized Nazi ideology in his work in Germany, even while the Nazis were still in power, through his philosophy of science and technology.

Nevertheless, he had much to regret about his involvement and never fully and appropriately recognized how much he was to blame for failing to resist and repudiate the Nazi regime. Some philosophers have viewed his theories as tainted; perhaps containing a hidden element of Nazi ideology. Three of Heidegger's students whom we will also discuss, Hannah Arendt (1906–1975), Herbert Marcuse (1898–1979), and Hans Jonas (1903–1993), German Jews who managed to escape Nazi Germany, were clearly influenced by and continued to make use of his theories and perspective. In my view, they knew far better than we can whether Heidegger's views had a hidden Nazi element, and their willingness to work with his ideas is good reason to think that, as much as we might condemn Heidegger personally for his involvement, we need not fear that his thought will lead us into fascism. In fact, I see good reason to think, in line with Heidegger's claim, that his later views, which we'll discuss, seem instead to analyze and criticize fascism, at least implicitly.

Science and Impiety

What seem to you to be the most obvious possible conflicts between scientific and religious views?

1. _____

2. _____

3. _____

4. _____

5. _____

Are there ways of making these religious and scientific views compatible?

_____

_____

_____

_____

_____

What kinds of religious views can't be made compatible with views based in science?

_____

_____

_____

_____

The Philosophy

"Science" is a relatively recent development of what used to be known as "natural philosophy," and philosophers of nature have run into resistance from religious perspectives from the very beginning. Socrates was sentenced to death for impiety, and it was claimed that he believed the sun was just a burning rock rather than the chariot of the god Apollo. Socrates claimed that he thought no such thing, but there were other ancient Greek philosophers who did.

We already discussed some of these Presocratic *physiologoi*—philosophers of nature—at the beginning of the previous chapter on Knowledge and Reality; theories like Thales's view that everything was water, or Democritus's claim that things are made out of "atoms." Anaxagoras (c. 500–c. 428 B.C.E.) was another one of these physiologoi, and he's the one who actually did claim that the sun was burning iron. He also worked on explanations of eclipses and the planets and came up with the idea that the moon shone by reflecting the light of the sun. Like Socrates, he was charged with impiety. For a society that we view today as sophisticated and philosophical, Athens was surprisingly prone to sentencing philosophers to death or exile for impiety.

Athenian government, though, was based in religion—Athens's legitimacy was said to come from the goddess Athena—and Greek religion was concerned with explaining nature, much more so than religious views today, which tend to view God as a creator and planner rather than an active force in the day-to-day workings of the world.

Religion has mostly retreated from making claims about planets, wind, crops, and natural history, but in ancient Greece the idea that we should try to figure out these things through reason and observation, rather than accepting the traditional stories, was still very dangerous. After all, if we start coming up with theories of nature, well, the next step might be trying to run the state based on reason and evidence rather than the traditional basis of civil authority in the will of the gods.

Heliocentrism

What role does mathematics play in science? Is mathematics just used to make sense of observations? Or does mathematics play a more active role in determining what those observations mean or even what sorts of things to make observations about?

_____

_____

_____

_____

_____

What's at stake in this issue—that is, what difference does it make whether mathematics plays a leading or a supporting role in scientific inquiry?

_____

_____

_____

_____

_____

_____

The Philosophy

Even though the most famous parts of Descartes's *Meditations on First Philosophy* are his radical, solipsistic doubt (How do I know I'm not asleep? Is an evil demon deceiving me by making me think that the world and other people exist?) and the *cogito* (I think, therefore I am), which helped him overcome that doubt, his actual *point* in the *Meditations* was to try to establish a scientific method that would allow "natural philosophy" to proceed with something like the same kind of certainty as mathematics.

Descartes thought that the problem was that science had depended too much on the senses and not enough on reason. Heliocentrism was one of the controversies of the day, and Descartes, like Galileo, believed that the earth revolved around the sun, rather than the other way around. The problem was that in commonsense observations, the earth below us certainly seemed to be stable and not hurtling through space, and the sun obviously moved in the sky. Furthermore, on the Church's reading of the Bible, it said clearly that the earth was fixed. The only factor in favor of heliocentrism was that it made for the more elegant mathematical model of the movement of the planets.

In the *Meditations*, Descartes tried to show that the senses weren't trustworthy, and that we needed a form of science based in reason and mathematics first, and observations only secondarily. Along the way, he also tried to provide proofs of God's existence and goodness as well as proof of an immortal human soul—after all, if his argument could prove these elements of faith *and* establish a mathematically based science, then the Church would be able to see that science (and heliocentrism) was compatible with faith.

There's Always Time for Mathematics

Mathematical knowledge is known immediately and permanently—once a proof is given, it is certain, and always certain. Scientific knowledge, on the other hand, seems to require a great many observations to establish, and scientific theories change over time, so the explanation of something today is always open for revision. Why is mathematical knowledge known with such certainty?

_____

_____

_____

_____

_____

Isn't it strange that we can come up with some mathematical proof in our heads and it turns out to be true in the world as well—and true with absolute certainty, and for all time? Why does math even work at all?

_____

_____

_____

_____

_____

The Philosophy

As mentioned in the last entry, Descartes thought that a mathematically based science could achieve something like the same kind of certainty as mathematics, and early modern scientists, like Isaac Newton (1643–1727), were much more likely than scientists today to talk about "laws" rather than just "theories" or "models." Of course, this didn't work out. But why not?

Immanuel Kant gave a very convincing explanation in his *Critique of Pure Reason*, published in 1781. As we discussed in the previous chapter on Knowledge and Reality, he argued that space and time aren't real things in the world outside of us, but are just the forms in which we perceive things— necessary conditions for the possibility of human experience. So any experience we will ever have will take place in space and time because those are the structures we use to experience things.

Geometry, he says, is nothing but an exploration of the concept of space. Space comes with a set of rules already in place— try to explain *why* the shortest distance between two points is a straight line!—and when we discover the relationships already there in the concept of space, we are discovering things that will always be true of everything we'll ever experience in the world, because we'll always experience it *in* space. Furthermore, because space is part of our internal workings, so to speak, it never changes, unlike things in the world, so proving something once is enough to make it true for all experiences by all humans for all time!

Arithmetic, similarly, is an exploration of time. When we add, we are saying in effect, "First this, and then that, and that makes two events." Everything else follows from there. So it's not accidental that we think of a "number line" going from infinite negative numbers to infinite positive numbers, with a zero in the middle, just as we think of time as taking place in one dimension, stretching infinitely into the past in one direction, and into the future in the other, with the present right in the middle.

The Raven Paradox

It seems as if a scientific theory can be supported by making observations that fit with the predictions hypothesized by the theory. Doesn't finding confirmation in experience serve as evidence in favor of a theory? For example, if your theory is that "all ravens are black," doesn't every black raven you see serve as support?

"All ravens are black" is logically equivalent to the claim that "all nonblack things are nonravens." (Seriously: "If it is a raven it must be black" means the same thing as "if it is not black it cannot be a raven.") This implies that, if looking at ravens and finding them to be black provides evidence in favor of the claim "all ravens are black," then looking at this page in this book and noting that it's white (and not a raven) provides evidence too. Does that make any sense? If so, how, and if not, what went wrong?

The Philosophy

The Raven Paradox comes from Carl Hempel (1905–1997), a German philosopher of science. Before we get into what to make of it, let's clear away a possible objection: We know enough about genetics to know that there must be some albino ravens—Google it, if ye doubt—and even if they didn't occur naturally, surely we could create one through genetic engineering, and if we just *defined* it as no longer a raven because it isn't black, then we'd be begging the question. A fair enough point. But Hempel is using a simple example to make a point about evidence and induction, so the specifics about genetics are really beside the point. You can substitute a claim about water being liquid at room temperature instead, if you want, and then we can talk about all the nonliquids that are not water at room temperature, and you're back in the same situation.

Philosophers have tried to dismiss the paradox in many different ways. But some philosophers, including Hempel himself, have accepted it. Why?

First, we might note that this seems silly because there's no *reason why* you'd go looking at pieces of paper to gather information about ravens, because there's no possibility of *dis*confirmation by looking around for various nonblack things to figure out if they're nonravens. But that doesn't mean that these other observations don't play a role in confirming the hypothesis—they just play a role in our background assumptions. Similarly, we might observe that there are a very large number of nonblack things compared to the number of ravens, so observing nonblack things that are also nonravens "counts for less" than observing ravens that are black.

Another possibility is to say the idea that scientific theories are confirmed through observation is just plain doomed. We already saw one argument along that line from Hume, in the previous chapter on Knowledge and Reality. But if scientific theories aren't supported by confirming observations, what *are* they supported by?

Falsification

Maybe induction and the idea of confirming a scientific theory are doomed. In this case, the most we could say for a scientific theory is that it hasn't been disproven (yet). Is that enough to explain how science progresses, and to reflect the strength of scientific knowledge?

_____

_____

_____

_____

Are there some kinds of things that could be true but could never even possibly be falsified—things that might be true, but if they were false, we would never know?

_____

_____

_____

Is there anything in the realm of scientific knowledge that couldn't be shown to be false, if it were false?

_____

_____

_____

_____

The Philosophy

Another German philosopher of science, Karl Popper (1902–1994), advanced a *falsificationist* view of scientific progress, which claimed, indeed, that scientific theories are never confirmed—in fact, the very idea that there can be evidence in their favor is wrong. A mountain of evidence that fits with a theory makes not a bit of difference in how certain that theory is. It might be the going theory, but it's just a theory, and a single decisive falsification is enough to bring it down. For example, Newtonian mechanics was a going theory for a very long time, and every single experimental observation (along with every single dropped apple!) for a couple hundred years seemed to confirm it. But experiments in the twentieth century finally brought it down, and none of that "confirmation" mattered.

The commonsense idea of scientific progress—that our theories are getting *better* in some way—is hard to account for in this view. Stranger yet, it seems as if a completely untested theory that someone just made up is just as "good" as a long-standing accepted theory. But there's something very appealing about the idea of falsification, in part because it does seem to identify, as Popper intended it to, a difference between scientific and nonscientific claims of knowledge. Scientific theories take risks; they make claims that can be tested and falsified, and this is why we value scientific theories! Pseudoscience, on the other hand, puts forth theories that are not falsifiable: Any seemingly contradictory evidence can be explained away from within the theory.

Popper talked about Marxism as such a theory, but today we might say the same thing about Libertarianism. In the one case, if the proletariat hasn't risen up, it's because they're enthralled by the false consciousness of capitalist ideology; in the other, if the free market isn't fixing everything yet, it's because we need yet more tax cuts and yet fewer regulations. In pseudoscience, even evidence seemingly against the theory is interpreted as confirmation.

Science and Pseudoscience

Let's look at Popper's "demarcation" theory, differentiating science from pseudoscience. What kind of evidence would falsify the theory of evolution? Is there any possible kind of fossil that evolutionary biology wouldn't simply treat as (perhaps puzzling) data to be accounted for from within the theory?

_____

_____

_____

What about the theory of intelligent design? Is it any more or any less falsifiable than the theory of evolution?

_____

_____

_____

_____

If you see a difference in falsifiability, is this enough to identify each theory —evolution and intelligent design—as either science or pseudoscience? If not, what other reasons might justify treating one as science and the other as pseudoscience?

_____

_____

_____

_____

The Philosophy

Falsifiability may not be enough to distinguish science from pseudoscience. What if we found ancient dinosaur bones along with a modern human skeleton, a saddle, and a bottle of whisky? This might be conclusive evidence that some specific conclusions based on the theory are wrong, and it would certainly be conclusive evidence that the past was awesome, but biologists wouldn't give up on the idea of evolution. Similarly, any evidence that seems to go against the idea of intelligent design can be accounted for from within the theory—for example, the "young earth" theory has been defended by claiming that fossils that appear ancient are a trick by the Devil to draw us away from faith.

On the other hand, evolutionary biology does make predictions that can turn out to be false—for example, that there must be a missing link in a particular evolutionary pathway, or that there are phylogenetic relationships between "related" species. When that link shows up, this provides some confirmation, and genetic testing could easily have falsified many hypotheses about whether species are related. Instead it has usually found the kind of genetic overlap that the theory predicted. Intelligent design, by contrast, is not only unfalsifiable as a whole, but does not clearly even make falsifiable hypotheses.

Imre Lakatos (1922–1974), a Hungarian philosopher of science, gives us another useful distinction. Good research programs are progressive—they expand in scope and precision. Failing research programs degenerate—they get too bound up in defending their core claims to do much but keep dealing with each next bit of challenging evidence. Evolutionary biology clearly has been and still is an expanding research program, whereas intelligent design has done little but try to cover the basics—and even here it does so not by making predictions that can be borne out, but simply by claiming "yes, but it could also have been God!" and looking for similar-seeming biblical passages.

Pessimistic Meta-Induction

Science, it has been claimed, works by inductive reasoning—finding a general truth though consistency in a number of cases. Consider, now, an inductive argument about the history of scientific induction: Every scientific theory except the current ones have been wrong. Therefore, we have good grounds to conclude that our current theories are wrong, too. What do you think; does that argument hold up?

_____

_____

_____

_____

_____

Is there anything fundamentally different about today's theories that would prevent this very consistent historical trend from applying to them as well?

_____

_____

_____

_____

The Philosophy

Yeah, that's pretty rough, isn't it? You know what else? I think this pessimistic meta-induction is right. We absolutely should assume that our current theories are wrong, just like all the previous theories. And the same thing can be said of the theories we come up with next, and the theories after that, and so on.

Philosophers who, like me, hold an *instrumentalist* view of science rather than a *realist* view are okay with this—in our view, scientific theories don't directly discover anything real, but are instead just models that can have predictive value. Pessimistic meta-induction is a problem on the realist view because it gives us reason to think that science will never "get it right"; on the instrumentalist view, this doesn't matter. Science is about prediction anyway, not reality.

We'll look at instrumentalism further in the next entries, but for now, let's consider a couple of other interesting arguments that are similar to pessimistic meta-induc-tion. Most people adopt the religious views of their families, and, as far as we know, we don't choose which family to be born into. So this means, in effect, most people are randomly assigned a religious view and should conclude that their beliefs are almost certainly wrong. Even on the assumption that there is a correct view, the odds of being born into it are very slim.

Swedish philosopher Nick Bostrom (1973–) offers this consideration: It seems likely that a sufficiently advanced human society will create computer-simulated worlds with virtual persons. With sufficient technological progress, these virtual worlds are likely to be cheap, and therefore plentiful. If you accept these assumptions, then it is reasonable to assume that you are living in a simulation—given these assumptions, there are far more virtual persons than real ones, and very numerous virtual worlds but only one real one. So, just based on the odds, it's a safe bet that you're just software running on a machine.

Knowledge and Know-How

Why is knowing the truth about reality valuable or important?

_____

_____

_____

_____

_____

_____

What difference does it make whether science is about discovering the nature of reality or, instead, is about coming up with models able to make increasingly valuable and accurate predictions?

_____

_____

_____

_____

_____

_____

The Philosophy

German-Jewish political theorist Hannah Arendt (1906–1975) was struck by how commentators, reacting to the launch of Sputnik in 1957, expressed "relief about the first 'step toward escape from men's imprisonment to the earth'." Just as once we conceptually escaped from determination by God the Father by turning to science rather than scripture to explain the world to ourselves, so too we now seek to escape from Earth the Mother—literally through space travel, and conceptually through genetically engineering ourselves. But for the sake of what, and in what direction, do we wish to escape? It seems that we fail to even ask.

Arendt claims we have traded knowledge for know-how. Science has progressed to a point where we can no longer explain or make sense of the meaning of our theories—in high-energy physics, at the least—and yet we can still run the math, and use the models to explore new frontiers of both science and engineering. Our ability to do things has outstripped our ability to make sense of their meaning, both in the sense that scientific models have departed from anything that makes sense in a human frame of reference, and in the sense that the broad impact of our scientific theories and engineering practices far outstrips our ability for (and interest in!) thinking through what they will change within ourselves and within our society.

If science is, as she thinks, just a matter of coming up with models that fit with the math and that have success in accurate prediction of experimental effects, then scientific knowledge is just a form of know-how; science itself looks like just a kind of technology—it doesn't tell us about reality, but instead tells us how to get the world to respond in one way or another. It may not be accidental that in a society that values this kind of science so highly, we are less and less in the habit of asking what is worth caring about and doing, as individuals and as a society, and more and more in the habit of uncritically expanding technology to its very limits.

Science and the Future of Nature

As we use nonrenewable resources or disrupt otherwise self-sustaining systems, as for example by depleting polar ice caps and causing sea levels to rise, we remove resources from people who are not yet born and, therefore, can't defend themselves from us. How could we change our government or our idea of responsibility to try to eliminate this form of "taxation without representation"?

_____

_____

_____

_____

_____

Imagine that, following some form of awful accident or war, there were only two living things left in the world: you, and a tree. Assume that you know somehow that, if left on its own, the tree will be able to reproduce itself, but that no self-aware, thinking being will ever exist again after you die. If it amused you to do so, would there be anything wrong with chopping down the tree?

_____

_____

_____

_____

_____

The Philosophy

Hans Jonas (1903–1993), another German-Jewish philosopher, noted that all of our ideas about morality and responsibility were formed in a context in which human action existed on a small scale and was dwarfed by the power of nature. Today, however, science and technology have entirely overtaken nature, and the choices we make, for the first time in human history, can have an effect on nature itself—and a devastating impact, slowly, through global climate change, or suddenly, as in the worries about genetically modified crops "going native," or questions about whether particle accelerator experiments might create a black hole, violently compressing the planet into a gravitational singularity.

Jonas concluded that we need to develop a new kind of morality to deal with our new kind of scientific and technological abilities. We have new obligations of knowledge. Once, the short scope of the possible impact of human actions fit well with our similarly limited foresight, but today the scope has grown to be entirely disproportionate to our foresight and our wisdom. Not only that, but a new question arises: Do we have any obligations to nature itself—not just persons or animals, but trees and islands and ecosystems—which has suddenly become dependent on our good judgment? The "last tree" question, originally from Richard Sylvan (1935–1996), is meant to give us a sense of what it would mean to think we might have an obligation to nature itself, as such.

The responsibility that our own science and technology demand from us seems impossible, especially in our age, when we seem so inclined to distraction and entertainment rather than serious contemplation. And yet it is in this age, when meditative thought is closing down in favor of know-how, that our know-how calls most clearly for meditative thought.

Only a God Can Save Us Now

Today, it seems as if we view the world as a set of mere objects available for our use. Is there something from the mythical and spiritual view of the world, from before the ascent of modern science, that we should try to recapture?

_____

_____

_____

_____

_____

Is this demythologized view of the world as a collection of objects for our use—especially in practices like mountaintop removal, hydraulic fracturing, and extracting energy from rivers and wind—connected to a loss of meaning in our lives, and a diminishing sense of the dignity and value of humanity?

_____

_____

_____

_____

_____

The Philosophy

Martin Heidegger (1889–1976) claimed that modern science and technology are based in a worldview that treats the world as "standing reserve"—as ready-made, so to speak, for our use. Starting even from Descartes in the seventeenth century, by calling "real" only those parts of nature that can be described mathematically and predicted according to exact and knowable laws, we have defined the world in terms of our ability to manipulate it and paved the way for the technological domination of nature, both practically and conceptually. Aspects of the world that don't fit into mathematical science are discarded as unreal. By defining the parts of the world that we can describe and have predictive know-how about as "reality," we have defined nature as if it were a technology. Even environmentalist claims work according to this logic: We think of trees as oxygen factories and ecosystems as complex machines and seek to manage these "technologies" of nature to fit human needs.

The destructive consequences of this perspective are obvious to us today, even more so than when Heidegger began writing on the topic in the 1940s. He said this dynamic is at work in our unprecedented environmental destruction, in the technological ordering and dehumanization of society involved in the bureaucratic regimentation of life in the twentieth century, and even in the mass production of murder through Nazi concentration camps. But for Heidegger, the most basic danger isn't these harms and horrors, but the possibility that this technological worldview may be permanent, that we may never have another way of encountering the world, and that the meaning of humanity and the world will be forever limited and impoverished. He said in 1976, at the end of his life, that "only a god can save us," by which he meant that only a new kind of source of meaning and value can open up this narrow technological perspective under which we live today.

CHAPTER 10

※

Aesthetics

The philosophical field of aesthetics includes a number of closely related concerns: our appreciation of nature, our appreciation of art, what makes an artwork a great work (or alternately, crap), the structure and logic of art, and what "progress" in art history means. As with every other chapter, there's much more going on in this area of philosophy than we can possibly explore. We'll get a nice sampling of issues, though, which will showcase the diversity of questions and concerns we might have with aesthetic experiences.

A quick note before we get going: just as the philosophy of science has focused on physics, perhaps too much, so too has aesthetic theory focused perhaps too much on visual art. I've made sure to address music in particular in these entries, though, for a couple of reasons. One is that I have a personal background in music theory and performance, so I've looked more into aesthetic theories of music than I might have otherwise. The other reason—and by far the more important one—is that music is part of our everyday lives, and even those who don't ever go out of their way to enjoy other forms of art are very likely to listen to music regularly, if not constantly. With MP3 players and muzak, music has become a constant element in our lives, arguably in a way and to an extent that no other form of art has ever before been infused throughout a society.

On the Standard of Taste

How does something get to be judged a great work of art?

_____

_____

_____

_____

_____

Can anything be a great work of art, if enough people say it is?

_____

_____

_____

_____

What if you—or what if everybody—no longer finds a work of art, traditionally recognized as a great work, compelling? Is it still a great work of art?

_____

_____

_____

_____

The Philosophy

It is said that *"de gustibus non est disputandum"*—or, in the slightly different English idiom, there's no accounting for taste. If someone doesn't care for lobster or pâté, there's not much that can be said to change her opinion. Are we right, though, to say that she is in some sense "wrong" in thinking they are not delicious? Surely those with refined palates appreciate these foods, and we would not be likely to choose someone who didn't to be a food critic, so there seems to be some basis for thinking that someone who doesn't appreciate fine foods isn't as good a judge of food, even though this puts us in the awkward position of saying sometimes that a dish is excellent even though we might not enjoy it.

We are in the same position with judgments of taste in art. David Hume's take on this strange situation starts with the observation that, while aesthetic judgment is a matter of personal feeling, our feelings are generally connected in some way to an objective state of affairs. When you burn your hand, for example, it is not because you are touching some pain that is there in the fire—the pain is in you, not the fire—and yet pain is surely a feeling connected in some way to the fire, and if someone else does not similarly feel pain when her hand is in the fire, you're inclined to say that there's something wrong with her.

Now, there's obviously more disagreement about which works of art are great than there is about whether fire will hurt your hand. In Hume's view this isn't a fundamental difference, but just a reflection of the fact that aesthetic appreciation is a subtle thing, and subject to influences by culture, religion, and our aesthetic training. We gain refined taste in art through long experience with great art, and through this process we can develop our aesthetic sense and become "true critics." And, circular though it may be, we identify great works as those that the true critics agree are great.

The Sublime in Nature

We don't usually find water or dirt terribly impressive. Why do we find our-selves enthralled by the Grand Canyon or the ocean?

_____

_____

_____

_____

I'm guessing you might have said that size matters. But is that enough to explain it? Do we find large numbers—the number "one million" for example—similarly enthralling? Why not?

_____

_____

_____

_____

We are in awe, also, of the forces of nature. Why do we find it thrilling to stand at the bottom of a powerful waterfall?

_____

_____

_____

_____

The Philosophy

Immanuel Kant considered aesthetic experiences, along with the other topics we've already heard about from him. Kant addressed at least something in almost every area of philosophy—and, amazingly, he did all of his important writing quite late in his career, publishing his first great work when he was in his fifties.

We don't talk much about the experience of the sublime anymore, but we're certainly familiar with the feeling: an overwhelming feeling of awe that we have standing before the ocean, or a towering cliff, or near the thunder of a waterfall, or in the midst of a near-terrifying violent storm.

In the experience of very large things (the "mathematically sublime"), we have a concept of the whole as a single thing, but we also know that it is made of individual bits. We can comprehend each individual bit, and understand what it is in normal terms, by imagining interacting with it, for example—but the whole thing is incomprehensibly large. So, for example, we can understand a bucket of ocean water—how large it is, what could be in it, and so on. When we look at the ocean, we try to extrapolate from that normal understanding of an amount of water to the incomprehensible and overwhelming multitude of bucketfuls of water. We are awed because although we cannot understand how much water there is before us, we are still able to see it and conceptualize it as a whole. It is the way that our conceptual ability outstrips our understanding that produces this feeling of wonder within us.

In experiences of the great force of nature in violent storms or waterfalls (the "dynamically sublime"), we are aware of how unimaginably powerful it is compared to us, and we feel awe in our ability to observe it without fleeing or being destroyed. As with the mathematically sublime, we stand in amazement of our own ability to deal with something on such a massive and overwhelming scale.

On the Judgment of Beauty

Is the experience of beauty just a personal feeling or a judgment about the beautiful thing?

_____

_____

_____

_____

_____

If it is a feeling, why do we expect others to agree with us? On the other hand, if it is a judgment, why can't we provide criteria and arguments to convince others to agree with us, or provide necessary and sufficient conditions for something to be beautiful?

_____

_____

_____

_____

_____

The Philosophy

Immanuel Kant began his theory of beauty by observing this very unusual dual character of aesthetic judgment: The experience of beauty is a feeling, but it is also a judgment about an object. And yet we can't simply define what it is based on, such that we can prove that it's there in the object. But we still claim that others are wrong if they disagree with our judgment of beauty!

Kant says that the enjoyment that we call "beauty" is found in the free play of our cognitive abilities. The thing that we call "beautiful"—I think it's easiest to understand this if you think of a painting or a symphony—has a rule-like structure but does not actually follow any strict and definable rules. No matter how complicated and intricate, no recipe can be given for how to make a work of art. The process of experiencing possible patterns emerge and depart, the play of order and meaning within something not determined by order or meaning, is what gives us the pleasure we call beauty. We might say today that beauty appears at the border of structure and chaos.

So, while the experience of beauty is just a feeling, it is based on an interaction between the beautiful object and the basic structures of human thought and understanding. Because those structures of the mind are universal, it makes some sense to claim that others ought to agree with us. This also explains how it can be both that beauty is a personal feeling and that the judgment that an object is beautiful really does identify something about the object, not just our merely personal reaction to it.

It's a surprisingly tidy solution to this apparent conceptual contradiction, but can it account for modern art? But then, maybe our reaction to and appreciation of modernist compositions is more complicated than just finding them "beautiful" . . .

Calm and Conflict

There's a story that Mozart once refused to get out of bed to receive a visitor. The man who had come calling went to the piano and loudly played a chord progression, ending on the dominant chord. Mozart, as predicted, couldn't stand it, and had to get up to play the tonic chord and resolve the tension by completing the chord progression. What is it like to experience dissonance as "tension," and why do we enjoy the movement from dissonance to consonance?

_____

_____

_____

_____

_____

What is "harmonious" about musical harmony?

_____

_____

_____

_____

_____

The Philosophy

Do you remember Arthur Schopenhauer, the guy we discussed at the end of Chapter 7: Aspects of the Self, whose theory was that the world is a manifestation of will that survives death? Schopenhauer played the flute. This has been a point of contention among some commentators, most notably, Friedrich Nietzsche. How can a man play the flute every evening, and yet claim that life is suffering and that all the evidence suggests that humanity is some sort of mistake? It's not an unreasonable question, but Schopenhauer's account of music helps us see why he, at least, didn't see any conflict between his beliefs and his practice.

Art, in Schopenhauer's view, is a way to express the human will so that it becomes external and available for contemplation. When we are able to observe the will in the artwork, separate from us, we are given a momentary rest from being driven by our own will and desires, and this rest is the pleasure that we take in art. By going through the movement of the will in the proxy of the artwork, our own wills are quieted, and we supplant the futile strivings and petty dramas of our own wills with a peaceful contemplation of the will, bare and separated from our own desires, in the work of art.

Music, Schopenhauer thought, was the purest art form, representing the will most directly. Other art forms are cluttered up by words, concepts, symbols, and images, but music is nothing but the movements of the will expressed in sound. While the proper goal in life is a negation of the will and a destruction of desire, music is able to give us temporary distance from the will and take us out, for a moment at least, from the vain striving and meaningless hustle and bustle that constitutes life.

Melodies, How Do They Work?

What are we hearing when we hear a melody? At each moment, we hear only one note or another....

_____

_____

_____

_____

Can any series of notes be a melody? If not, why not?

_____

_____

_____

Head over to YouTube and listen to a twelve-tone composition, like Arnold Schoenberg's (1874–1951) Piano Concerto op. 42. What do you think—do you still agree with your previous view about what makes a melody?

_____

_____

_____

_____

The Philosophy

Phenomenologists—roughly speaking, philosophers of the what-it's-like of experience—have addressed musical listening, and brought fascinating insights to what seems to us to be a very simple thing, but which is really anything but.

In hearing a melody we are, it is true, hearing isolated notes in succession, but we experience the melody rather than the notes. The French phenomenologist, Maurice Merleau-Ponty (1908–1961), compared the melody to a film. In the film we see only isolated pictures, each of which is gone before the next arrives, and yet we experience the movement and change, not any of the images as an image. In the same way, in listening, we experience the *gestalt*, or the system of elements as a system, and experience the elements within it only as parts of what appears to us essentially as a whole.

Each note, then, as we experience it, is experienced in the context of the notes that come before—but this context is not produced through memory. As Merleau-Ponty pointed out, if we *remembered* the previous notes, we would be recalling something; instead we continue to *feel* the previous notes even though we are no longer (literally) hearing them. Another phenomenologist, Edmund Husserl (1859–1938), called this *retention*. The experience of the previous note is retained in our current experience of the current note, and the note we hear is set against the background of those notes we retain—those notes that we no longer hear, but which we continue to feel rather than merely remember.

There is a similar process of *protension*, wherein we "feel" the notes that we have not yet heard, but which are implied in the note we currently hear—this is what got Mozart out of bed in that story. The melody emerges from the notes we hear placed against the notes we *retain*, and containing the notes we *protain*, even when, as in Schoenberg, the notes that actually follow are different from the ones we "heard" before we heard them. The melody, like all experience, is a blurred mix of past, present, and possible futures.

Listening under Late Capitalism

You almost certainly believe that pop music reached its high point when you were seventeen. Almost everyone believes this, no matter when they were seventeen and no matter what sort of tacky nonsense they were listening to that year. (I still have an unjustifiable love of third-wave ska, for example.) What does this say about what our judgment of quality in music is based on?

We'd be likely to judge someone who, today, listens pretty much exclusively to '70s disco, '80s New Wave, or '90s Neo-Swing. What does it say about our relationship with music that music can become embarrassing?

The Philosophy

German-Jewish philosopher Theodor Adorno (1903–1969) wrote deep and complex analyses of popular culture, focusing most of all on music. In an influential essay, "On the Fetish-Character in Music and the Regression of Listening," he claimed that our engagement with music is characterized, on the one hand, by encountering music as a commodity, and on the other hand as an element of personal identity and comfort (regression and repetition in the Freudian sense, where, like children, we demand the same thing over and over again). Notably missing in both these elements is the actual aesthetic experience of the music.

The commodity character of music is revealed in a number of ways. In Classical music, orchestras perform only particular famous pieces, because they are the ones that everyone knows—because they are the ones that orchestras perform—and a great many works at least as valuable are almost entirely ignored. The consumer displays the tickets proudly and whistles the catchiest motif in the subway car, showing that his concern is having acquired the cachet and social meaning of having had the experience, not the experience itself.

In popular music, style and fashion form the basis of our experience. Adorno writes that our rage against music that isn't up-to-date, that has become "corny," shows that our previous "enjoyment" of this music was only a pseudopleasure of consumption and amusement rather than a real aesthetic pleasure.

Adorno doesn't discuss our attachment to the musical styles of our youth, but it fits in perfectly with his analysis—he might have said that we form a lasting attachment to this music because it has become bound up with our self-identity and serves as a safe memory to which we can retreat at moments of uncertainty, freeing ourselves from the burden of experiencing change and growth. Hearing it gives us the empty calories of musical macaroni and cheese. In these ways, we see that listening today has little to do with music.

The End of Art

For each of the following, answer these questions: Was this art? Is this art? If someone did this today, would it be art? Why would it be art or not-art?

- *In 1917, Marcel Duchamp (1887–1968) submitted a urinal to an art exhibition, and signed it "R. Mutt."*

_____

_____

- *In 1921, Alexander Rodchenko (1891–1956) produced a series of three paintings. One panel was red. Another was yellow. The third was blue.*

_____

_____

- *In 1964, Andy Warhol (1928–1987) silkscreened a wood block to look like a box of Brillo brand soap pads.*

_____

_____

- *In 1971, Chris Burden (1946–) performed a piece entitled "Shoot," in which he had someone shoot him in the arm.*

_____

_____

- *In 1991, Damien Hirst (1965–) produced a work, "The Physical Impossibility of Death in the Mind of Someone Living," which consisted of a fourteen-foot tiger shark in formaldehyde.*

_____

_____

The Philosophy

In his theory of artistic progress, American philosopher Arthur Danto (1924–) adopted a general view of the progress of art from German philosopher G. W. F. Hegel (1770–1831) and used it to provide a detailed analysis of modern and postmodern art. In Hegel's original theory, art has progressed through different eras, very roughly speaking, by a gradual decrease of concrete and imitative elements in art and an increase in the expressive and ideal (in the sense of "being about ideas") elements. In Greek sculpture, the statue is viewed as the god itself, and serves a symbolic function. In Classical art, most clearly in painting, realistic and literal representation is combined with expressive content, properly reflecting in beauty the nature of humanity as both free and material. In Romantic art, most clearly in poetry and music, the inner nature of humanity is emphasized. In Hegel's view, art is *about* the representation of humanity, and so symbolic art is not yet art, whereas Romantic art represents a disintegration of art from its Classical realization.

Danto extends and changes this historical view, and his version is much less abstract and much more plausible. In his view, art progresses by breaking apart the limits of what can be art. At first art was imitative and took on an expressive function. The imitative aspects of art were broken down, and art became that process by which we see that each stylistic and conventional constraint on what "counts" as art is in fact unnecessary to art. I'll show you what I mean. In Impressionism, the actual presence of the paint comes forward in the viewer's experience of the work, deemphasizing the importance of representation. In Modernism and Abstract Expressionism, the process is carried further. In found art, the process of artistic creation itself is shown to be unnecessary. Today, according to Danto, we are "after the end of art," because art, understood as this process of breaking down its own constraints, has finished. Today, it seems, there are no rules about what "counts," except that art must be a further development and what used to be art cannot be art today.

CHAPTER 11

---✳---

Death

In Chapter 8: Knowledge and Reality, we said that while the entries in that chapter dealt specifically and narrowly with those topics, in an important sense every entry in the book, at its basis, is really about questions of knowledge and reality. That's certainly true when we speak of "basis" in an abstract, conceptual sense, but if we speak of the basis in practical experience instead, a case can be made that it is death that forms the basis of every other question in the book.

Some questions, like those about God, can be traced back to a fear of death and its meaning. Science and the quest for knowledge can be viewed as an attempt to control and predict the world, perhaps a kind of sublimation of our impossible desire to control and predict our departure from the world. Questions of how to live—whether of happiness, justice, morality, or art—gain their force from our awareness that we only seem to get the opportunity to do so once, so we'd better get it right while we can.

Here we focus on four topics dealing with death in different ways:

* Voluntary death
* Abortion
* Declarations of war
* The confrontation between our search for meaning and the fact of death

I'll also take this moment to say goodbye. I hope these explorations have been fun and valuable, and I'm very excited to hear back from readers about where these questions have taken you. In writing this book, I've tried to avoid thinking that what you might gain from it is what I put into it. Instead, I've tried always to remind myself that the truest and most valuable forms of learning and change take place in the world and in your life, and to write what I have written in an attempt to provide focusing lenses and pathways to explore, rather than to supply "content." That is more true here than anywhere else. Ultimately, only death can teach us anything about death.

The Death of Socrates

What do you believe happens to you after death? (Or, at least, what's your working hypothesis?)

_____

_____

_____

_____

_____

_____

Are you afraid of death? Why or why not?

_____

_____

_____

_____

_____

The Philosophy

Socrates's death is almost certainly the most famous death in the history of philosophy. In 399 B.C.E. after he was found guilty of impiety and being a corrupter of the youth, the prosecution asked for the death penalty. According to the structure of trials in ancient Athens, the defense was able to propose an alternate sentence, and the jury would decide between the two proposed sentences. Socrates showed a surprising lack of concern for his fate, proposing that he be sentenced to free meals in the Prytaneum, an honor usually given to Olympic victors. (He did backpedal a bit, and eventually offered to pay a fine of 30 *minae*, estimated to be equivalent to around $40,000 in today's dollars.) The jury chose the sentence of death—and did so by a wider margin than they had chosen the verdict of guilty! In explaining his lack of concern for his life, Socrates said that he had been given by the gods to Athens as a gadfly, to awaken the city into wakefulness through his constant biting inquiry. And so to agree to stop his challenging questioning or to propose that he leave town (exile is probably the alternate sentence that the jury was expecting from him) would amount to deserting his post, and, like a virtuous soldier, he would rather face death by staying in his post than flee out of fear for his life.

He also said that death is said to be either nothingness or a migration of the soul. In the first case, then to die is to enter a sleepless dream, which is a pleasant thing. In the second case, then to die is to have the opportunity in the afterlife to speak with the greatest of men: Orpheus! Hesiod! Homer! He ended his address by saying, "The hour of departure has arrived, and we go our separate ways, I to die, and you to live. Which of these two is better only God knows."

Suicide

Suppose that someone, not depressed, but in pain and facing unavoidable dete-rioration from an incurable disease, wishes to die. Would there be anything wrong with her suicide? Why or why not?

_____

_____

_____

Suppose she needs help to end her life. Assuming for the moment that it would be acceptable for her to do so on her own, would there be anything wrong in assisting in the process?

_____

_____

_____

Suppose she is not depressed, not in pain, and not facing disease, but is simply weary of living. Would her suicide be wrong?

_____

_____

_____

Would your assistance in this circumstance be wrong?

_____

The Philosophy

David Hume considered the issue in an essay too controversial for him to publish during his lifetime. The topic was even more taboo then than today. In England, not long before Hume wrote, suicide was so looked down upon that those who were found guilty of it were not allowed to be buried in the same graveyards as others, were buried at night without mourners, and had their property seized by the state rather than being passed down through inheritance.

Hume began his consideration by claiming that if suicide is a crime, it must be a crime against God, against our neighbors, or against ourselves. The first is most commonly discussed today as the idea that only God should decide the hour of our deaths. Hume reasons that God established various limits on our behaviors and actions, yet certainly made it possible for us to end our lives. But are we perhaps upsetting the course of events established by God in accordance with His plan? If God's plan includes our choices, then this can't be the case—and, we might add, if God's plan doesn't include our choices, then we are as surely going against His will if we save someone's life, and we don't regard that as wrong.

As to our duties to our neighbors, we can note that we surely have a duty to give back to a society that supports us. But we don't think there's anything wrong with becoming a hermit—the hermit no longer contributes to society, but doesn't depend on society either, and so owes nothing to it. Suicide is no different than becoming a hermit, in this respect.

Finally, regarding our duty to ourselves, Hume says, "I believe that no man ever threw away life, while it was worth keeping. For such is our natural horror of death, that small motives will never be able to reconcile us to it." And so, we can be assured that anyone who chooses it chooses it for significant reasons and based on serious interests.

The Human, the Animal, and the Person

Is someone who is brain dead a person?

_____

_____

_____

What sorts of interests—desires, hopes, plans, and preferences—are the brain dead able to have? How do those interests enter into our consideration of how to treat the brain dead?

_____

_____

_____

Is a fetus a person? At what point does it become one?

_____

_____

_____

What sorts of interests is a fetus able to have? How do those interests enter into our consideration of how to treat the fetus?

_____

_____

_____

The Philosophy

Australian philosopher Peter Singer begins his consideration of the morality of abortion by making a crucial distinction: Just because something is a person does not mean that it's human, and just because something is a human does not mean it is a person. We can easily imagine a nonhuman being that would have the same kind of moral worth as a human person, if it has the same traits that make us persons. Roughly speaking, these probably include self-awareness, the ability to have plans and long-term interests, and possession of values, goals, and ideals. Similarly, there are humans who are clearly not persons: for example, the brain dead, or anencephalic fetuses, who never develop brains. To say that humanity grants moral worth is speciesism—a form of prejudice directly parallel to racism. Instead we should say that our special moral status comes from our personhood, not from our genetic makeup.

If that's true, then there's a kind of moral spectrum among animals, who have greater moral weight as they have greater capacities to have interests, preferences, and plans. We talked about this view of animal rights back in Chapter 3: Morals—here, we can apply it to different kinds of humans as well. Someone who merely persists vegetatively, like the brain dead or the anencephalic, has no self-awareness, is incapable of having interests, and clearly does not require our moral consideration.

The healthy fetus, similarly, can be treated with the same kind of consideration as we would treat any other being with similar capabilities. Even for late stages of pregnancy, a fish is perhaps closest: The fetus may be able to experience pain, but has at most a very limited self-awareness, and no plans or desires. Killing anything shouldn't be done without reason, but if the fetus has similar moral worth to a fish, then justifying the choice to abort a pregnancy—while it is always a difficult decision for the mother—doesn't require us to worry much about whether we are doing any great wrong to the fetus.

A Future Like Ours

Perhaps the fetus isn't a person, but it is certainly a potential person. What bearing does that potential for becoming a person have on our treatment of the fetus?

_____

_____

_____

_____

_____

_____

Why is it wrong to kill an actual person—for example, you?

_____

_____

_____

_____

_____

_____

The Philosophy

Some philosophers have responded to the argument that abortion is morally permissible because the fetus is not yet a person by extending the moral value of persons to *potential* persons. It's a position that makes some intuitive sense, but the details don't work out well. We don't usually give rights based on potentiality—you, for example, are potentially the president, but don't expect access to any briefings on issues of national security. Don Marquis (1935–), an American philosopher, put forth an anti-abortion argument that argues that the fetus's future may make abortion wrong but does not resort to questionable claims about potential personhood.

He begins by asking what it is that makes killing an adult person, like us, wrong. It isn't the pain, because painless killing is still terribly wrong. It isn't our current desire to be alive, because killing someone in her sleep, or while she's suicidally depressed, is still terribly wrong. It is wrong, Marquis thinks, because it deprives us of a valuable future, in which not only will we realize our goals and experience pleasures, but we will find new and further things to desire and take pleasure in. And here's the thing: The fetus has a future like ours. And we can see that it has a future like ours apart from any particular concept of "person" or any extension of that concept to "potential person." So, he argues, if the fetus has a future like ours, that should make abortion wrong in the same kind of way that killing an adult is wrong.

It's a very strong argument, but I'm not convinced that a fetus can be wronged by the loss of a future that, of course, never ends up existing, and of which it is never aware. In my view, we treat killing seriously not because the person killed suffered a wrong—the victim is, after all, beyond all harm at that point—but because the rest of us *currently* don't want to be killed. This brings the wrongness of killing away from the metaphysics of futures that no longer exist (did they ever exist?) and back to the concrete reality of our own plans, desires, and hopes.

The Violinist

What do we mean when we talk about a "right to life"?

_____

_____

_____

_____

Does a right to life just mean that we shouldn't kill people, or does it obligate us to go out of our way to save the lives of others?

_____

_____

_____

_____

If it does produce an obligation on our part, how great a sacrifice are we obliged to make to save someone's life?

_____

_____

_____

The Philosophy

American philosopher Judith Jarvis Thomson also took an approach to the issue of abortion that avoided the issue of personhood (and potential personhood). She simply *assumed* the personhood of the fetus, and tried to show that the right to an abortion still followed.

Imagine you are kidnapped by a society of music lovers and wake up in a hospital bed attached to a famous violinist. They explain to you that the virtuoso has a rare condition that will kill him unless he is able to recover by making use of someone else's kidney for nine months. You are the only person compatible. Are you obligated to stay?

She thinks our intuitions here should be clear. Surely, it would be a generous sacrifice to agree to stay with him for nine months and allow him to live, but you would be entirely within your rights to refuse and to leave, even though it means he would die.

Thomson's "violinist example" is widely recognized as making a very strong case for the right to abortion in the case of rape. Extending the argument to other cases is trickier, considering that in a pregnancy resulting from consensual sex, in a departure from the analogy, the woman has done something related to her attachment to this being that is now dependent upon her.

Thomson considers one interesting idea about how the argument could be extended. Suppose a burglar breaks into your house. Does he have a right to live there now? Of course not. Okay, easy enough so far. What if an innocent person falls through your window? No, he wouldn't have a right either. Well, then, Thomson asks us to imagine that "people-seeds drift about in the air like pollen, and if you open your windows, one may drift in and take root in your carpets or upholstery. You don't want children, so you fix up your windows with fine mesh screens, the very best you can buy. As can happen, however, and on very, very rare occasions does happen, one of the screens is defective; and a seed drifts in and takes root." Does that innocent person-seed gain a right to your house?

Preemptive War

Is war justified when one of our country's allies is being threatened? How serious does the threat need to be?

_____

_____

_____

_____

_____

_____

_____

Is war justified to prevent a country that has declared itself to be our enemy from becoming a threat? (That is, assuming that the country is not currently a threat.)

_____

_____

_____

_____

_____

The Philosophy

Just war theory has a long tradition, going back at least to St. Thomas Aquinas and St. Augustine. Traditionally, these are the conditions that have been viewed as necessary for a just declaration of war:

* That there be a just cause, based on a country's aggression against another nation or against its own people
* That all other options in halting that aggression, short of war, have been exhausted
* That there be a fair chance of success (for otherwise war would only be a useless shedding of additional blood)
* That the good that would come from military success outweigh the harms created by the war itself

From this traditional view, the first Iraq war seems quite justifiable: Iraq's invasion of Kuwait was obviously an aggressive act, and there were clear reasons to take military action immediately in defense of a sovereign nation. (Of course, Iraq was a sovereign nation as well, but in just war theory, a state that engages in military aggression loses its right to be left alone.)

The second Iraq war is much more troubling, because it was not justified by an act of aggression. It is true that Iraq had "waged war" on its own people, especially the Kurds, but the war was not justified by appeal to this valid reason for humanitarian intervention—instead, the idea that Iraq was developing weapons of mass destruction was used as a justification.

This argument for a right to wage preemptive war is deeply troubling for just war theory. Michael Walzer (1935–), probably the most prominent just war theorist today, argues that preventative war is justified only when a country has made both hostile declarations and concrete preparations for war. The idea of going to war to prevent a state from even *becoming* a threat in the first place, however, seems very unjust—there are other options short of war (for example, sanctions) if there has been no act of aggression, and the evils prevented by the war are uncertain, whereas the harms of going to war are significant and certain.

The Path to Peace

Assume for the moment that Iraq actually had been developing weapons of mass destruction in 2003. Given the massive destructive force of WMDs, would going to war against Saddam Hussein's regime have been the right choice, even if it was unjust?

_____

_____

_____

_____

_____

_____

Is deterrence through building and maintaining a strong military a good path to peace? Why or why not?

_____

_____

_____

_____

_____

The Philosophy

In the abstract, preemptive war does seem clearly unjust. The enemy is not a threat and may not ever become one. Such a war violates the sovereignty of a nation that has taken no aggressive action. The doctrine of preemption undermines international peace, because it seems to offer a blanket justification for any nation to wage war against any other nation with a stated hostility to another nation—it would justify any ally of Iran or Israel in attacking the other on the basis of their often-stated hostility. And what about India or Pakistan or their allies? Or the United States or North Korea? But the extreme threat posed by WMDs seems to many to be sufficient reason to say that a doctrine of preemption is necessary today, even if it is unjustified.

Immanuel Kant's view on war is as strict as his view on lying, which we discussed previously in Chapter 3: Morals. *Any* kind of aggression, including aggressive stances short of war, is unacceptable in his view. Even simply maintaining a standing army,

he argues, leads toward war and is unacceptable. If a neighboring nation has a large military, we feel we need a large military as well, just in case that neighbor *becomes* hostile one day. Of course, they feel the same way about our military, and an arms race quickly begins between two nations, even if they are not hostile. Eventually, the logic of preemption seems to demand waging war: Attack the other (nonhostile) nation before it becomes too strong to resist (if it became hostile).

Kant admitted that it seems unrealistic to say that we should not keep ourselves ready to defend ourselves. But, he said, the reality is the other way around: It is unrealistic to think that preparing for war will bring peace. It is true that a country that does not prepare for war makes itself vulnerable, but it is also true that the only way we will ever have peace is for all nations to refuse to prepare for war. The high road, in this case, is the only road that leads to the desired destination: Perpetual peace.

A Death of Your Own

What does your own death mean to you?

_____

_____

_____

_____

_____

_____

How does thinking about your death change how you think about your life?

_____

_____

_____

_____

_____

_____

The Philosophy

In Martin Heidegger's first great work, *Being and Time*, published in 1927, our awareness of our own deaths plays a special role in his phenomenology—again, that's an analysis of the "what it's like"—of human life. We are "thrown" into the world; we only gain self-awareness and a sense of personal agency and choice once our lives are already well underway. We find ourselves *within* language, because we have little understanding or memory of ourselves or the world prior to learning to speak and think in words. We are thrown into a system of tools, technologies, and practices of living—we only gain any control over who we think we are long after we have internalized an understanding of how things work, and what people do. In all, we are "thrown into *the One*"—a claim that makes much more sense than it seems to at first.

We are "thrown into," that is, we find ourselves always already within the bounds of, "the One," that is, the expectations about "what one does" and "what one doesn't do." Who is "the One" in these kinds of claims, anyhow? Well, it's us, for the most part; which is to say, we usually act out the roles we find ourselves in rather than creating our own paths and self-interpretations.

But your awareness of your own death can shake you out of it. It is true that "one dies," but that's hardly relevant to what death means to *you*. *You* will die. No one can do it for you, and doing what "one does" provides no guidance, comfort, or familiarity. Death—*your* death—is a radical, permanent, individual break. This opens up an awareness of authenticity: That your death is yours alone, and that you face it alone without support from what "one" does, requires you to define yourself as an individual and see the inauthenticity of the One as an arbitrary convention into which you have been thrown. The fact that your death is ineliminably *yours* calls you forth to make your *life* yours as well.

The End of All Things

Not just us, today—although that's true as well—but all living beings able to think and care will die. Not only individually, but it seems as a whole as well; eventually the earth itself will be rendered sterile and barren, leaving unimaginable eons of nothing but dead rocks floating in the empty vacuum of space, far outweighing this fleeting moment where self-awareness and meaning flickered briefly in the cold and eternal night. What's the point? What's the point of trying? What's the point of anything, when it will all come to nothing in the end?

_____

_____

_____

_____

_____

_____

_____

_____

_____

The Philosophy

In his 1873 essay, "On Truth and Lies in a Nonmoral Sense," Friedrich Nietzsche wrote:

Once upon a time, in some out of the way corner of that universe which is dispersed into numberless twinkling solar systems, there was a star upon which clever beasts invented knowing. That was the most arrogant and mendacious minute of "world history," but nevertheless, it was only a minute. After nature had drawn a few breaths, the star cooled and congealed, and the clever beasts had to die.

One might invent such a fable, and yet he still would not have adequately illustrated how miserable, how shadowy and transient, how aimless and arbitrary the human intellect looks within nature. There were eternities during which it did not exist. And when it is all over with the human intellect, nothing will have happened.

Sigmund Freud (1856–1939) wrote a commentary on death and meaning, very closely connected to this little story from Nietzsche. Now, we don't usually think of Freud as a philosopher, but he admitted that Nietzsche was an early influence on him (although he doesn't admit the full range of that influence), and even quotes Schopenhauer, to whose work Freud's was also clearly indebted.

In his 1915 essay "On Transience," Freud recalled a conversation with a young poet, during a walk through the countryside. There's reason to believe that this poet, whom Freud did not name, was Rainer Maria Rilke (1875–1926), whose stunningly beautiful and achingly tragic poetry fits well the poet's role in the story. The poet's enjoyment of the countryside was prevented by his thought that it was transient; that winter would soon bring death upon its lush splendor and cease its futile exuberance.

Freud wrote that the "proneness to decay of all that is beautiful and perfect" drives us either to the despondence of this poet or to wish fulfillment in the refusal to believe that death is the end. Using what is called a "hermeneutics of suspicion," Freud states that the belief in the immortal soul is too much in line with our desires to think that our tendency to believe in it could be based in anything but our own desires. It is too convenient an answer to be convincing. But Freud also rejected the poet's withdrawal from emotional attachment to a world of merely fleeting beauty. Transience does not destroy value, but should intensify it, as the scarcity of a good usually does. As he wrote, "a flower that blossoms only for a single night does not seem to us on that account less lovely."

Freud speculates that the poet is mourning in advance for what will be lost, making every attachment and enjoyment painful, due to the knowledge that the object of this appreciation and admiration is doomed to pass away. As Freud wrote about elsewhere, after making an emotional investment in a love object—when the beloved dies, the world seems impoverished, because the value placed upon the love object is then missing from the world. Mourning, the process of letting go of the lost and beginning to reinvest value in the world, is painful and difficult, but ceasing to make these attachments in the first place is a poor solution.

After the Great War, in which European nations who believed themselves civilized descended again into hideous and inhumane bloodshed of a kind that they had thought was a thing of the past, Freud himself went through a kind of mourning; it seems he wrote his essay on transience to reflect on this. Even though World War I showed how fragile and temporary, how transient the achievements of civilization and progress in human morality and rational action are, still, this should not be a cause for depression or hopelessness. Rather it is a reason to value these cultural achievements all the more highly.

We may perhaps say the same thing of this brief flicker of thought and meaning within a universe whose farthest reaches in time and space seem to contain only emptiness. Such a rare and fleeting flower—so beautiful and so temporary it makes one cry.

APPENDIX

A Timeline of Philosophers Discussed

The following is a timeline of the thinkers mentioned in this book, outlining their major contributions to philosophy.

The Presocratics

While many of the Presocratics did live before Socrates's time, as the title might imply, several of the so-called Presocratics were around at the same time as Socrates. Plato even wrote a dialogue of an encounter—perhaps fictional, but quite possibly historical—between Parmenides and Socrates. But the Presocratics are "before" Socrates in a logical sense: Their concerns with metaphysics, mathematics, and natural philosophy influenced Socrates and Plato, and they were not influenced by the turn that Socrates and Plato made toward questions of value; of virtue, justice, and beauty.

THALES OF MILETUS (c. 624–c. 546 B.C.E.): The earliest of the Presocratics, Thales believed that the cosmos was composed of a single substance, and that substance was water. He was an accomplished mathematician as well, applying deductive logic to problems of geometry.

ANAXIMANDER OF MILETUS (c. 610–c. 546 B.C.E.): A pupil of Thales, he believed that nature acts according to immutable laws and that these are capable of being studied and classified. He believed the cosmos was built of an endless primordial mass, from which all visible phenomena are derived.

ANAXIMENES OF MILETUS (585–528 B.C.E.): The third of the trio of famous Presocratic philosophers of the Milesian school, Anaximenes believed that the fundamental substance from which everything is made is air. He used this principle as the basis of a system of cosmology.

PYTHAGORAS OF SAMOS (c. 570–c. 495 B.C.E.): Although he's best known for his theorem (which he may not even have formulated), Pythagoras is equally important as a philosopher. His concept of a group of thinkers influenced Plato, as well as his notion that ultimately philosophy can be based on mathematics.

HERACLITUS OF EPHESUS (c. 535–c. 475 B.C.E.): He argued that the universe is characterized by constant change; he likened it to a river, saying, "you cannot step twice into the same stream"—the stream, as a stream, is not the waters which constitute it at any moment, but the change of waters itself.

PARMENIDES OF ELEA (c. 515–c. 450 B.C.E.): Founder of the Eleatic school of philosophy, Parmenides claimed that change is impossible, and must be an illusion. The famous paradoxes of his student **Zeno of Elea** (c. 490–c. 430 B.C.E.) are meant to prove this by showing that simple, everyday things are impossible, and that therefore the world we experience must be an illusion. In the most famous, we imagine Achilles running a race against a tortoise, which has a head start. By the time Achilles catches up to where the tortoise was, the tortoise will have moved a bit further. By the time Achilles gets to where the tortoise was then, the tortoise will again have moved a bit further. And so on. Therefore, Achilles can never catch up to the tortoise.

ANAXAGORAS OF CLAZOMENAE (c. 500–c. 428 B.C.E.): He argued that the universe, composed of an infinity of small fragments, was brought into

214

existence and order through the power of *Nous*, loosely translated as "Mind."

DEMOCRITUS OF ABDERA (c. 460–c. 370 B.C.E.): Sometimes called "the Father of Science," Democritus is also noted for his theory that everything is made of indivisible particles, which he named "atoms" (a theory derived from his master **Leucippus** (first half of the fifth century B.C.E.).

DIOGENES OF SINOPE (412–323 B.C.E.): A member of the philosophical school of Cynicism, which argued that true happiness lies in living a life of virtue, lived in accordance with nature.

Classical Philosophy

Following Socrates, philosophers in the Golden Age of Greek philosophy began to concentrate more on questions of ethics and justice, and philosophy branched out beyond the earliest questions of knowledge and reality.

SOCRATES (469–399 B.C.E.): Teacher of Plato and one of the most important of the early philosophers, Socrates focused primarily on ethical questions. He was charged with and executed for corrupting the minds of the young and denying the gods of the state.

PLATO (429–347 B.C.E.): Pupil of Socrates, Plato is considered among the most important —if not *the* most important—of Greek philosophers. In *The Republic* he put forth his theory of justice and the theory of the Forms; in other works he discussed questions of truth, reality, beauty, virtue, and memory. Among the pupils in his school, the Academy, was Aristotle.

ARISTOTLE (384–322 B.C.E.): Having been a pupil of Plato, Aristotle developed a philosophy that differed in many respects from his former master, emphasizing experience and observation rather than abstract reasoning and argument. He lectured extensively at his school, the Lyceum, and his pupils compiled extensive notes that were published as his works. He served as teacher for a time to the future emperor Alexander the Great.

EPICURUS (341–270 B.C.E.): His philosophy of Epicureanism holds that happiness derives from an absence of fear and pain and from living in a state of self-sufficiency. His thought was significantly influenced by Democritus, whose atomism he adopted with an important modification: Epicurus claimed that atoms could sometimes "swerve," which allowed him to claim that we are not subject to causal determinism.

EPICTETUS (55–135): One of the late Stoics, Epictetus believed that we can only be happy by letting go of all events beyond our control, and care only for those things that are up to us to determine. It is perhaps indicative of the broad applicability and appeal of Stoic teachings that the two most well known of the Roman Stoics are Epictetus, who was a slave, and Marcus Aurelius, who was an emperor.

AUGUSTINE OF HIPPO (354–430): Augustine, who began life as a pagan, is among the most famous of early converts to Christianity, under the influence of his mother. He wrote several important works, including a biography titled *The Confessions*, and *The City of God*, a discussion of the relationship between the works of God and the works of man.

Medieval Philosophy

Following the decline of Rome, the tradition of so-called "European" or "Western" philosophy was carried on in Islamic and Judaic traditions, often outside of Europe. Major Islamic and Jewish philosophers of this time include **Al-Farabi** (c. 872–950), **Ibn Sina** (**Avicenna**) (c. 980–1037), **Ibn Rushd** (**Averroës**) (1126–1198), **Mosheh ben Maimon** (**Moses Maimonides**) (1135–1204), and **Levi ben Gershon** (**Gersonides**) (1288–1344). As these traditions began to connect back to the Christian tradition, Europe emerged from its "dark ages" and Christian philosophy emerged as a major tradition, dealing with a wide range of ethical, metaphysical, and political issues.

ANSELM OF CANTERBURY (1033–1109): The most famous early bishop of the seat of English Christianity, Anselm also constructed one of the best-known arguments for the existence of God: the ontological proof.

THOMAS AQUINAS (1225–1274): A major figure in Scholastic philosophy, he attempted to reconcile Christian doctrine with Classical philosophy. This reflected a renewed interest in Christian medieval Europe in the works of Greek philosophers, especially those of Aristotle, influenced by the Islamic and Jewish philosophers and commentators who had preserved, continued, and adapted the Greek tradition.

The Scientific Revolution

In the age of **Galileo Galilei** (1564–1642), **Isaac Newton** (1643–1727), and other important natural philosophers, philosophy formulated what is known today as science, continued to advance dialogues from the ancients and from religious philosophy, and explored connections (and divergences) between science and religion.

RENÉ DESCARTES (1596–1650): Although best remembered for "I think, therefore I am," Descartes was also a mathematician and scientist of note as well as an originator of rationalism, the theory that knowledge is derived from reason and not from sense experience.

JOHN LOCKE (1632–1704): A major influence on the eighteenth-century creators of the American republic, Locke is among the most important Enlightenment thinkers, which included other prominent English and Scottish philosophers such as Adam Smith, David Hume, and Francis Bacon. An empiricist, Locke claimed that the mind was a blank slate (tabula rasa) and that all knowledge derived from experience.

GOTTFRIED LEIBNIZ (1646–1716): Among other accomplishments, Leibniz was the creator of differential calculus (at the same time as Isaac Newton). He codified many of the laws of formal logic and suggested that everything exists for a necessary purpose, known to God. In Voltaire's 1759 novel *Candide*, he was satirized as the tutor Pangloss.

The Enlightenment

Eighteenth-century philosophy placed reason at the center of human endeavors and exam-ined questions by the light of rationality, while at the same time exploring the limits of human knowledge.

DAVID HUME (1711–1776): A representative of the Scottish Enlightenment, Hume held an extreme version of empirical thought that rejected rationalism. According to him, all statements must be verifiable by experience; otherwise they are either merely logically true or false or meaningless.

ADAM SMITH (1723–1790): A moral philosopher and economist. Though he was a champion of capitalism, Smith would have been horrified at today's notions of finance capitalism and corporate greed. Instead, his book *The Wealth of Nations* argued that true prosperity arises from fair competition between producers, enhanced by a division of labor among workers.

IMMANUEL KANT (1724–1804): Kant published important works dealing with metaphysics, ethics, aesthetics, and political philosophy, including his immensely influential *Critique of Pure Reason*. In this work he brought together the rationalist and empiricist traditions, demonstrating that some forms of knowledge must emerge from the mind alone (pure reason) rather than sense experience— but that these forms of knowledge only apply to human experience, not reality in itself.

WILLIAM PALEY (1743–1805): Paley is the originator of the watchmaker argument for God's existence (sometimes called the teleological argument). He was a leading exponent of Utilitarian thought.

Nineteenth-Century Thought

Philosophers in the nineteenth century attempted to come to grips with the impact of the industrial revolution and the increasing urbanization of society.

G. W. F. HEGEL (1770–1831): One of the most important nineteenth-century philosophers, Hegel's theory of dialectical change had an immense influence on later philosophers, particularly Karl Marx.

ARTHUR SCHOPENHAUER (1788–1860): In the words of P. G. Wodehouse, "a grouch of the most pronounced description," Schopenhauer's pessimistic thought was influenced by Indian mysticism. He believed that the world is governed by Will, which constantly seeks satisfaction and is constantly frustrated in its quest. He viewed Hegel, his contemporary, as a charlatan, and purposefully scheduled his lectures at the same time as Hegel's so that students would be forced to choose between them. Schopenhauer attracted few students, and did not teach again, although he became influential through his writing, and ultimately gained fame through a series of essays written for a general audience, his *Parerga and Paralipomena.*

JOHN STUART MILL (1806–1873): Building on the work of the philosopher and legal reformer **Jeremy Bentham** (1748–1832), Mill popularized Utilitarian theory, the idea that happiness is defined as the greatest good for the greatest number. Mill also wrote significant works on democratic theory, economics, and logic, and authored an important early feminist work, "The Subjection of Women." While his wife, **Harriet Taylor Mill** (1807–1858), wrote little under her own name, J. S. Mill wrote in his autobiography that she was an uncredited contributor to much of his work.

SØREN KIERKEGAARD (1813–1855): A Danish philosopher and theologian, Kierkegaard is often viewed as the founder of religious existentialism. He argued that true understanding comes from contemplation of the inner self and that external and totalizing systematic theories cannot capture the meaning of the individual.

KARL MARX (1818–1883): Among the most influential philosophers who ever lived, Marx observed, in a well-known passage that "philosophers have only interpreted the world, in various ways; the point is to change it." Marx was the creator of scientific socialism and the spiritual father of the communist movement of the nineteenth and twentieth centuries. Much like Adam Smith's relation to many contemporary forms of capitalism, Marx would have been horrified to see many of the things that have been done in his name.

FRIEDRICH NIETZSCHE (1844–1900): One of the great tragic figures of philosophy, Nietzsche wrote on a variety of philosophic and literary subjects

before lapsing into insanity and an early death. The tragedy he suffered did not end with his death: He became among the most misunderstood of philosophers, largely because of purposeful and politically motivated misinterpretation. His sister edited some of his work to support her own anti-Semitic views after he became incapacitated, and he was taken up by the Nazis as a philosophical foundation—despite that his negative comments about Judaism were intended to prey upon the prevalent prejudices of the time to open up a criticism of Christian hypocrisy, that he had personal relationships of care and admiration with Jews, and that he harshly criticized nationalism, and consistently disparaged the Germans. His criticisms of "woman" and femininity have often been taken as misogyny, where they are at least as easily read as a challenging sort of feminism, and he had close working relationships with women and female scholars, whom he clearly respected. He is often taken to be simply anti-Christian, although, most notably in *The Antichrist*, he took care to defend the person of Jesus against what he viewed as the perversion and hatred of the Church. As a personal smear, it has also been claimed that his illness was due to syphilis, while it seems that he suffered from an illness contracted while serving in the military as a medic.

W. K. CLIFFORD (1845–1879): A British mathematician and philosopher, he argued that the only reality is mind, made up of simple units (equivalent in the physical world to atoms), which he called "mind-stuff."

WILLIAM JAMES (1842–1910): A prominent member of a famous family (his brother was the novelist Henry James), he was a leading psychologist as well as a philosopher. He was an important figure in the development of American Pragmatism, along with **Charles Sanders Peirce** (1839–1914) and **John Dewey** (1859–1952). Among his most important works are *The Principles of Psychology, The Will to Believe and Other Essays in Popular Philosophy, The Varieties of the Religious Experience, Pragmatism: A New Name for Some Old Ways of Thinking,* and *Essays in Radical Empiricism.*

Twentieth-Century and Contemporary Philosophy

Thinkers of the twentieth and twenty-first centuries have had to deal with some of humanity's greatest crises, including the Holocaust, nuclear weapons, political and social revolution, and the growth of technology. Philosophy as an academic field also underwent significant changes in the late nineteenth and early twentieth centuries, as more and more areas of philosophical inquiry gave rise to independent disciplines. Psychology, sociology, economics, and anthropology, among other disciplines, became their own fields during this time, although the most fundamental and foundational questions in all of these areas remain philosophical. Analytic philosophy also emerged during this time, out of a post-Kantian rejection of metaphysics.

SIGMUND FREUD (1856–1939): While his name is obviously much more closely associated with psychology, Freud was working within the German philosophical tradition, and was clearly influenced by Nietzsche and Schopenhauer, strongly influencing, in turn, philosophers including Herbert Marcuse, **Jacques Derrida** (1930–2004), **Gilles Deleuze** (1925–1995), and **Félix Guattari** (1930–1992). His works are read in philosophy courses today, particularly *Totem and Taboo, The Future of an Illusion,* and *Civilization and Its Discontents.*

EDMUND HUSSERL (1859–1938): Founder of phenomenology, which Husserl described as a "return to the things themselves"—an attempt to recover an understanding of human experience from underneath the layers of theory and cultural conceptualizations through which we normally understand experience. Husserl, a German Jew, was replaced at the University of Freiburg by his student, Martin Heidegger, under pressure from the Nazi regime.

MARTIN HEIDEGGER (1889–1976): Heidegger's legacy is clouded by his political association with Nazism, but he is still recognized as among the most important philosophers of the twentieth century. His phenomenological inquiry focused on the study of Being, which to him was the fundamental subject of philosophy. His later work on science and technology made him a foundational figure in the philosophy of technology.

HANNAH ARENDT (1906–1975): A student of Heidegger's, with whom she had a troubled romantic relationship, Arendt, a German Jew, was forced to flee Germany and eventually settled in the United States. Arendt wrote broadly in political philosophy, but had particular concerns with violence and the rise of totalitarianism. Her coverage of the trial of Adolph Eichmann in Israel in 1962 gave birth to the expression "the banality of evil."

HANS JONAS (1903–1993): A friend of Hannah Arendt and a student of Edmund Husserl and Martin Heidegger, Jonas was another of many German-born Jewish philosophers forced to leave their country in the face of Hitler's rise to power. He wrote extensively on ethics, arguing that one should act so that the effect of one's actions is compatible with genuine human life.

HERBERT MARCUSE (1898–1979): Marcuse was also a German-Jewish student of Edmund Husserl and Martin Heidegger, and one of a number of philosophers, critics, and social thinkers associated with the Frankfurt Institute for Social Research (colloquially known as the Frankfurt School). Those associated with the institute attempted in various ways to fuse Marxism, Freudianism, and philosophy into interdisciplinary social theory. After escaping Germany, Marcuse settled in the United States, and in later years, while teaching at Brandeis and the University of California, he was adopted by the hippies and became an idol of the American New Left.

THEODOR ADORNO (1903–1969): Like Marcuse, Adorno was an associate of the Frankfurt School, and a Jew forced to flee Nazi Germany. He was a music critic, philosopher, and the coauthor of a massive psychological study, *The Authoritarian Personality*, published in 1950, which examined American test subjects who showed some of the traits of German fascists.

KARL POPPER (1902–1994): An Austrian of Jewish descent, Popper emigrated to New Zealand in 1937, and then took a position at the University of London after the war. Popper became well known for his work in philosophy of science and political philosophy, and was knighted by Queen Elizabeth II in 1965.

CARL HEMPEL (1905–1997): A philosopher of science, Hempel was associated with the Berlin Circle and Vienna Circle—groups of philosophers working on logical positivism, an important movement in analytic philosophy which claimed that propositions which do not admit of verification are meaningless.

JEAN-PAUL SARTRE (1905–1980): Sartre is among the most famous of twentieth-century philosophers because of his existentialist writings, his novels and plays, his political activity, and his long-term relationship with Simone de Beauvoir. In 1964 he refused a Nobel Prize in literature.

SIMONE DE BEAUVOIR (1908–1986): Through her book *The Second Sex,* she was one of the founding theoreticians of the modern feminist movement, as well as being an acclaimed novelist and a significant existentialist philosopher.

MAURICE MERLEAU-PONTY (1908–1961): A leading French philosopher, although less of a household name than Sartre or de Beauvoir, both of whom he studied alongside and worked with before their relationship suffered a political falling-out. Merleau-Ponty was a phenomenologist who emphasized the importance of the body and of language in structuring experience and thought.

MILTON FRIEDMAN (1912–2006): Friedman is the founder of what has become known as the Chicago School of economists. An articulate champion of the unrestricted free market against what he saw as the dangers of big government, he is much beloved of political conservatives. He served as economic consultant to several governments, including the dictatorship of Augusto Pinochet in Chile in the 1970s.

ALBERT CAMUS (1913–1960): An absurdist novelist, political activist, playwright, and philosopher, Camus is among the most widely read of modern philosophers through such novels as *The Stranger* and *The Plague.* Born in French Algeria, Camus confronted issues of colonialism in his work and had a lifelong concern for human rights that led him to work in favor of pacifism and against capital punishment; to write for the French Resistance newspaper *Combat,* alongside Sartre, during the Nazi occupation; to join the French Communist party; and eventually to leave the French Communist party, becoming an anarchist. Tragically, he died young in an automobile accident only three years after receiving the Nobel Prize for literature.

J. L. MACKIE (1917–1981): An Australian philosopher, working primarily in the fields of ethics and metaphysics, as well as the philosophy of religion. He claimed that all moral values are purely relative and that we cannot deduce the existence of an objective set of moral guidelines.

PHILIPPA FOOT (1920–2010): An influential British ethicist, she played a leading role in contemporary virtue ethics and originally formulated the much-debated "trolley problem." She was also an important early supporter and trustee of Oxfam.

JOHN RAWLS (1921–2002): An American philosopher and leading figure in moral and political philosophy, he is best known for his *A Theory of Justice,* which created new direction and vitality in philosophical debate about distributive justice.

IMRE LAKATOS (1922–1974): A Hungarian philosopher of mathematics and science who adapted Hegelian dialectic to develop a theory of the progress of science and mathematics, he fled the Russian invasion of Hungary and settled at the London School of Economics, where he worked with Karl Popper.

ARTHUR DANTO (1924–): An American philosopher and art critic, he has become a major figure in aesthetic theory, most notably through his ideas about "the end of art" and the sociological and conventional definitions of art in what he calls "the artworld."

EDMUND GETTIER (1927–): An American philosopher, he is best known for a paper, "Is Justified True Belief Knowledge?" published in 1963. The thesis of the paper, influenced by the work of **Ludwig Wittgenstein** (1889–1951), was that not all true and justified beliefs can be called "knowledge."

HARRY FRANKFURT (1929–): An American philosopher dealing with moral philosophy and the philosophy of mind. His 1986 paper "On Bullshit" was later published as a book and became a bestseller.

JÜRGEN HABERMAS (1929–): A German sociologist and philosopher of political theory, he built off the Marxist tradition, as well as incorporating the social thought of Max Weber and others to construct a theory of communication.

JUDITH JARVIS THOMSON (1929–): An American moral philosopher, she is widely known for her philosophical defense of abortion.

DON MARQUIS (1935–): An American moral philosopher well known for his article, "Why Abortion is Immoral," which put forth the "deprivation argument": that abortion is wrong because it deprives the fetus of a future like ours.

MICHAEL WALZER (1935–): An American philosopher and editor of the magazine *Dissent*, a liberal journal. He works primarily on political and moral philosophy, and is a prominent communitarian and just war theorist.

ALBERT BORGMANN (1937–): A German philosopher and longtime professor at the University of Montana, his work in philosophy of technology develops Heideggerian ideas in a much more practical and concrete direction, advancing the idea of the "device paradigm" as a way of understanding how particular forms of technological life sacrifice meaning and value in human life for efficiency.

DONNA HARAWAY (1944–): A leading feminist philosopher of science and technology, she has written a number of books and articles concerning gender, race, primates, companion animals, science, and technology. Her most famous work is the essay, "A Cyborg Manifesto: Science, Technology, and Socialist-Feminism in the Late Twentieth Century."

PETER SINGER (1946–): An Australian philosopher writing on moral and political philosophy, he's a prominent utilitarian ethicist and advocate of animal rights. Singer's 1975 book, *Animal Liberation*, was influential to Ingrid Newkirk and Alex Pacheco, who founded PETA (People for the Ethical Treatment of Animals) in 1980. Singer's views on abortion and euthanasia have made him a sometimes-controversial speaker, leading to protests, mostly based on a misunderstanding of his positions.

MAXWELL JEREMIAH ORANGEFELLOW (1998–): A cat of the Orangefellow clan, holding a Master's in Kitteh Studies. Like Socrates, he has produced no written work, but from what I can tell by living with him, he seems to have things pretty well figured out.

Index

Note: Page numbers in **bold** indicate questions to be answered. Page numbers in *italics* indicate biographical sketches.